The Mermaid's Ocean Adventure

A Coloring Book for kids and adults

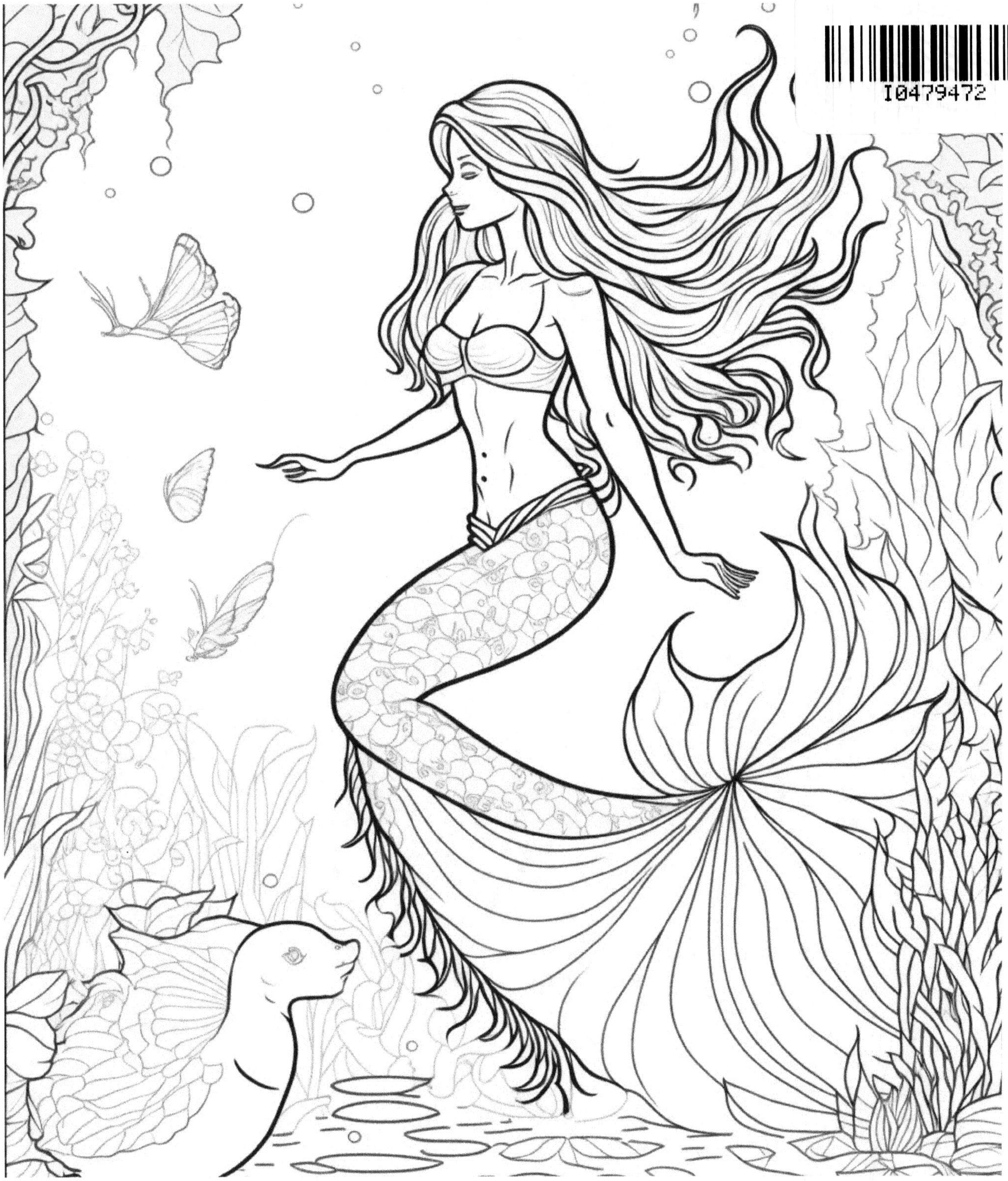

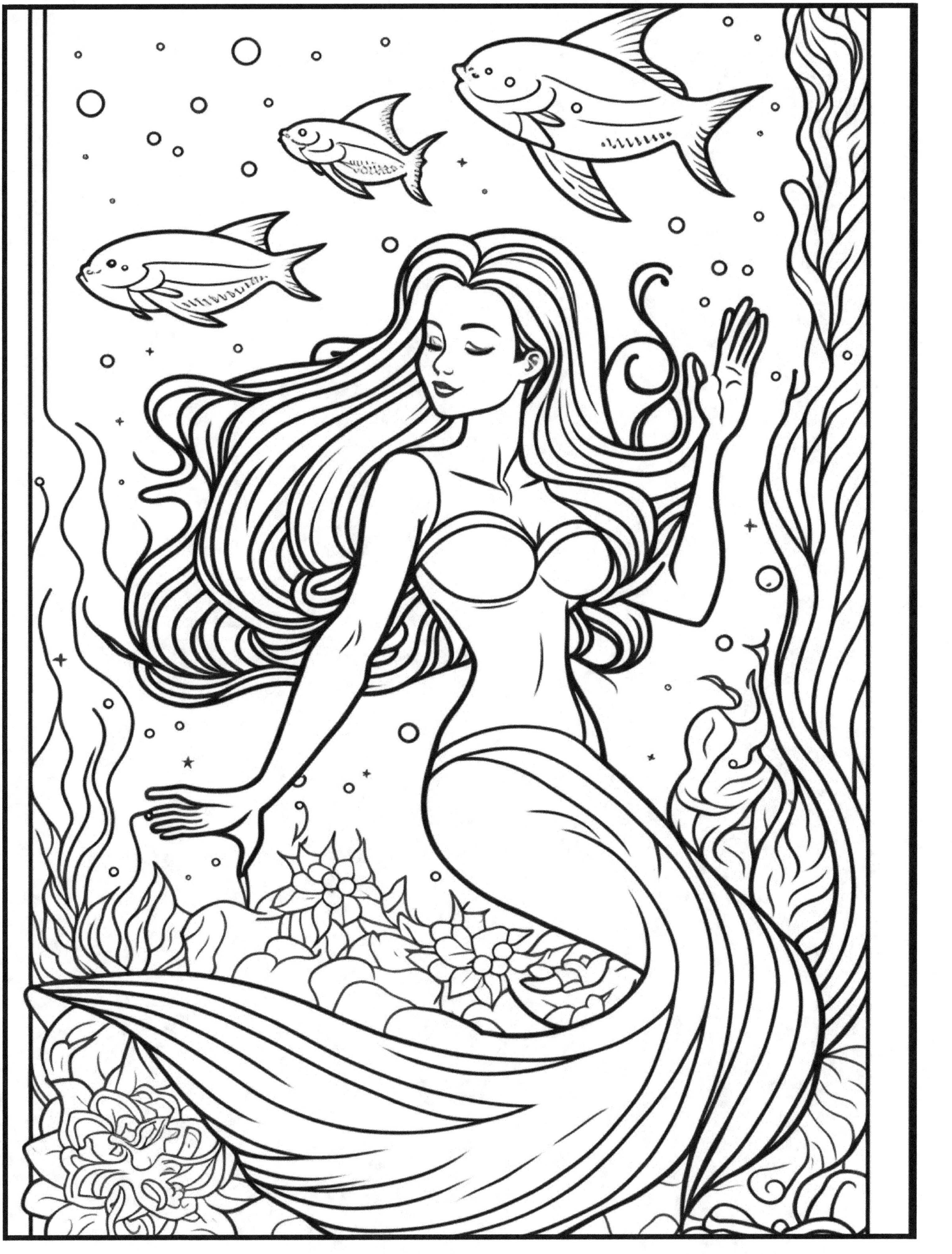

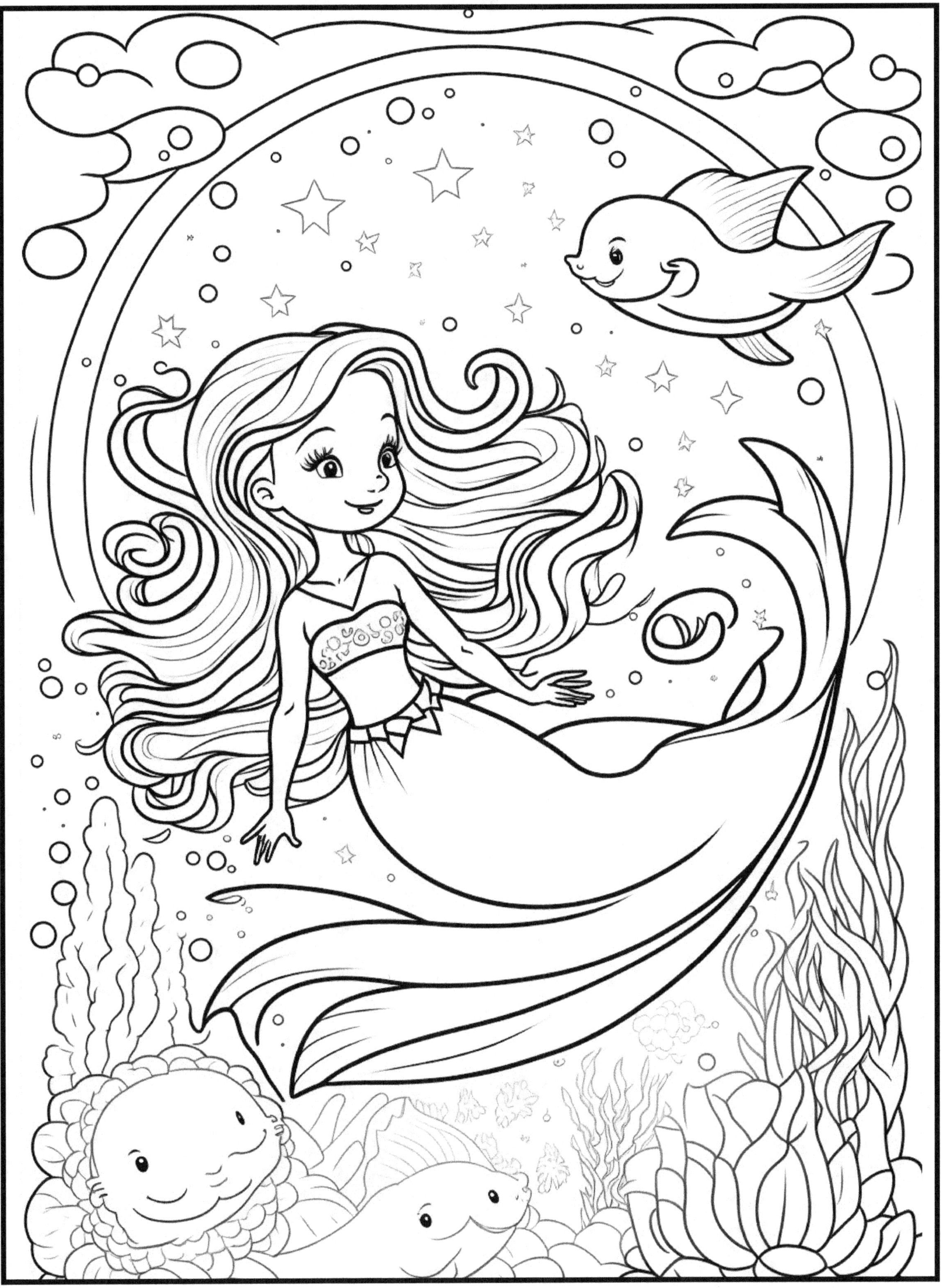

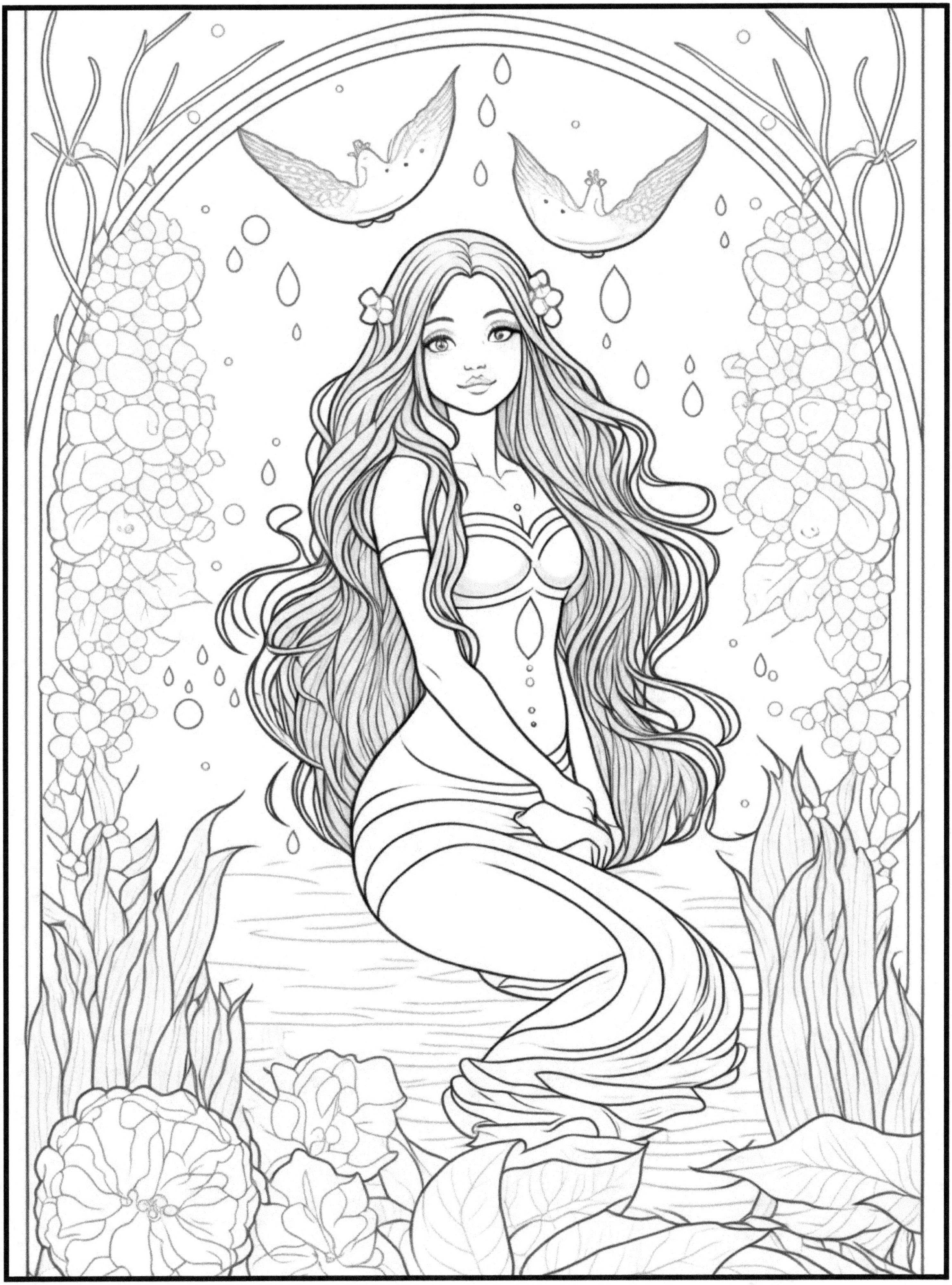

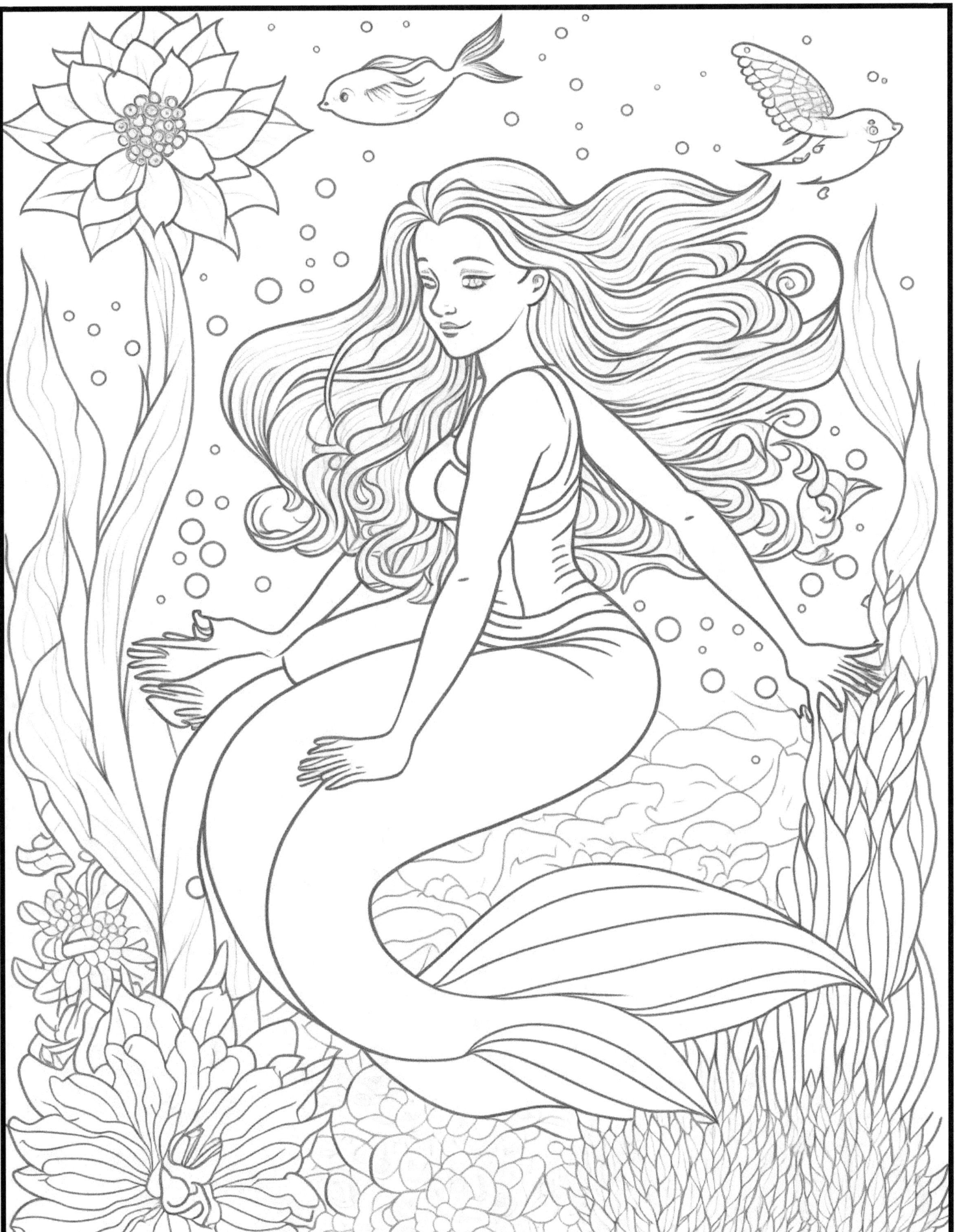

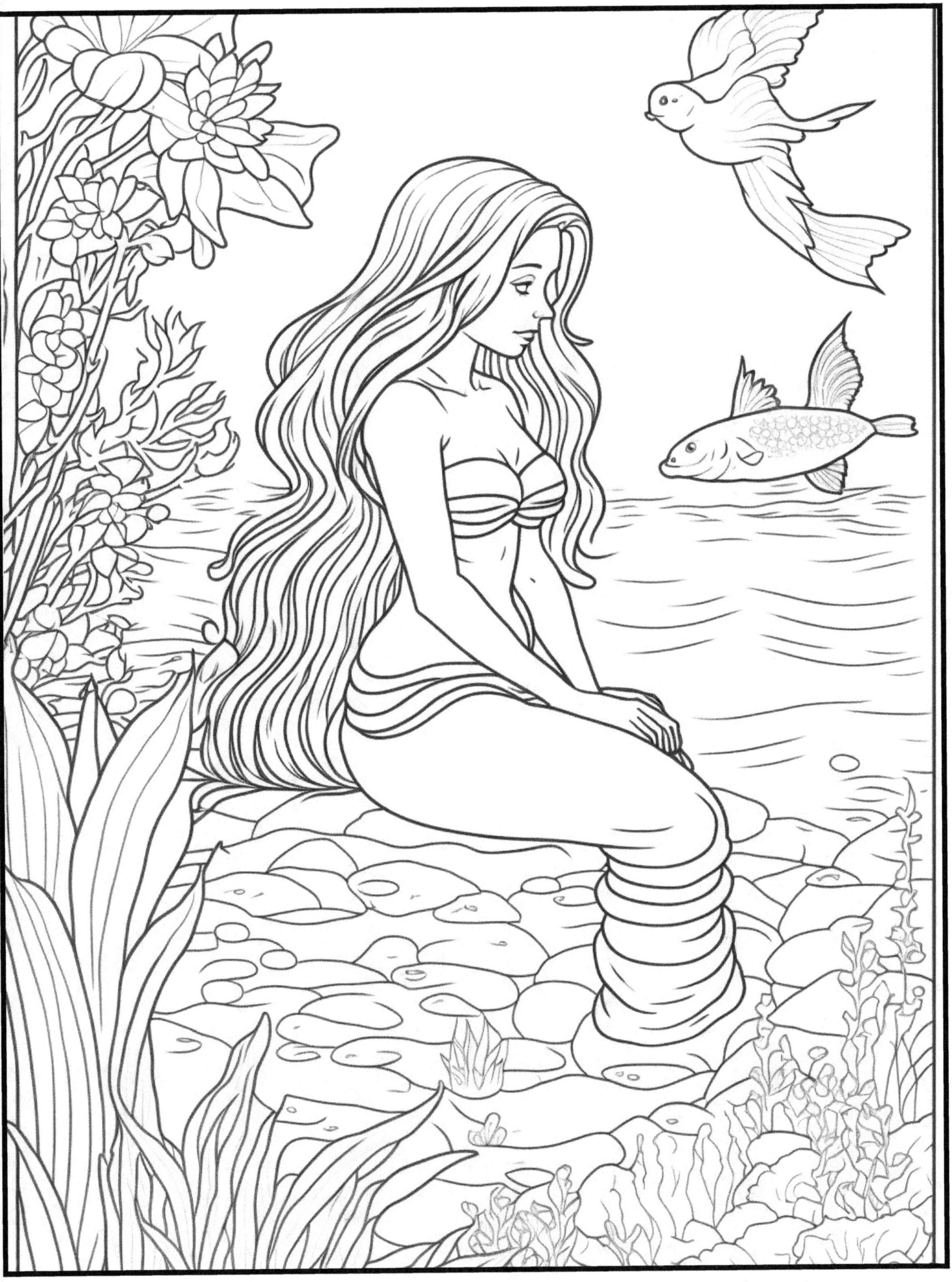

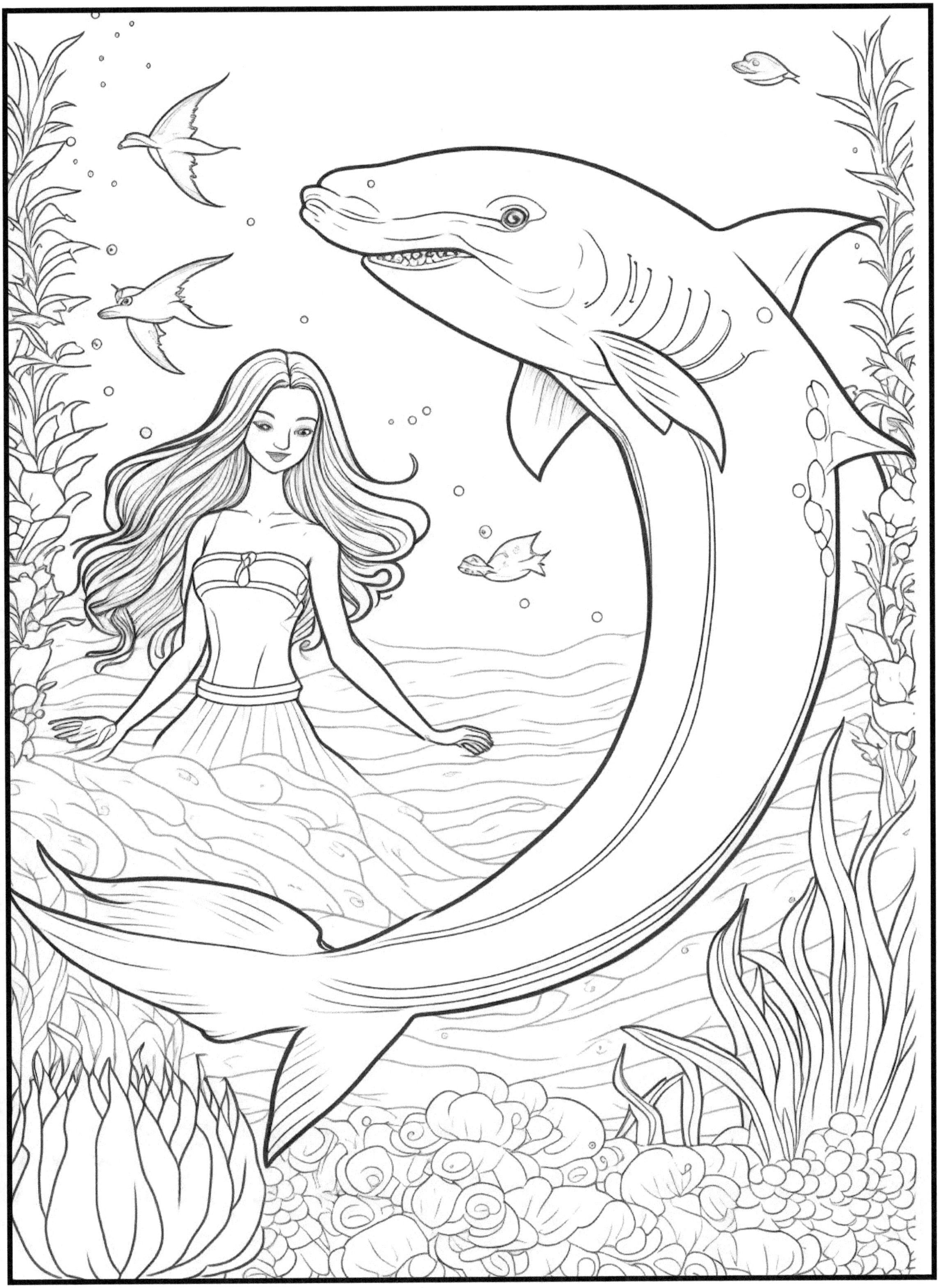

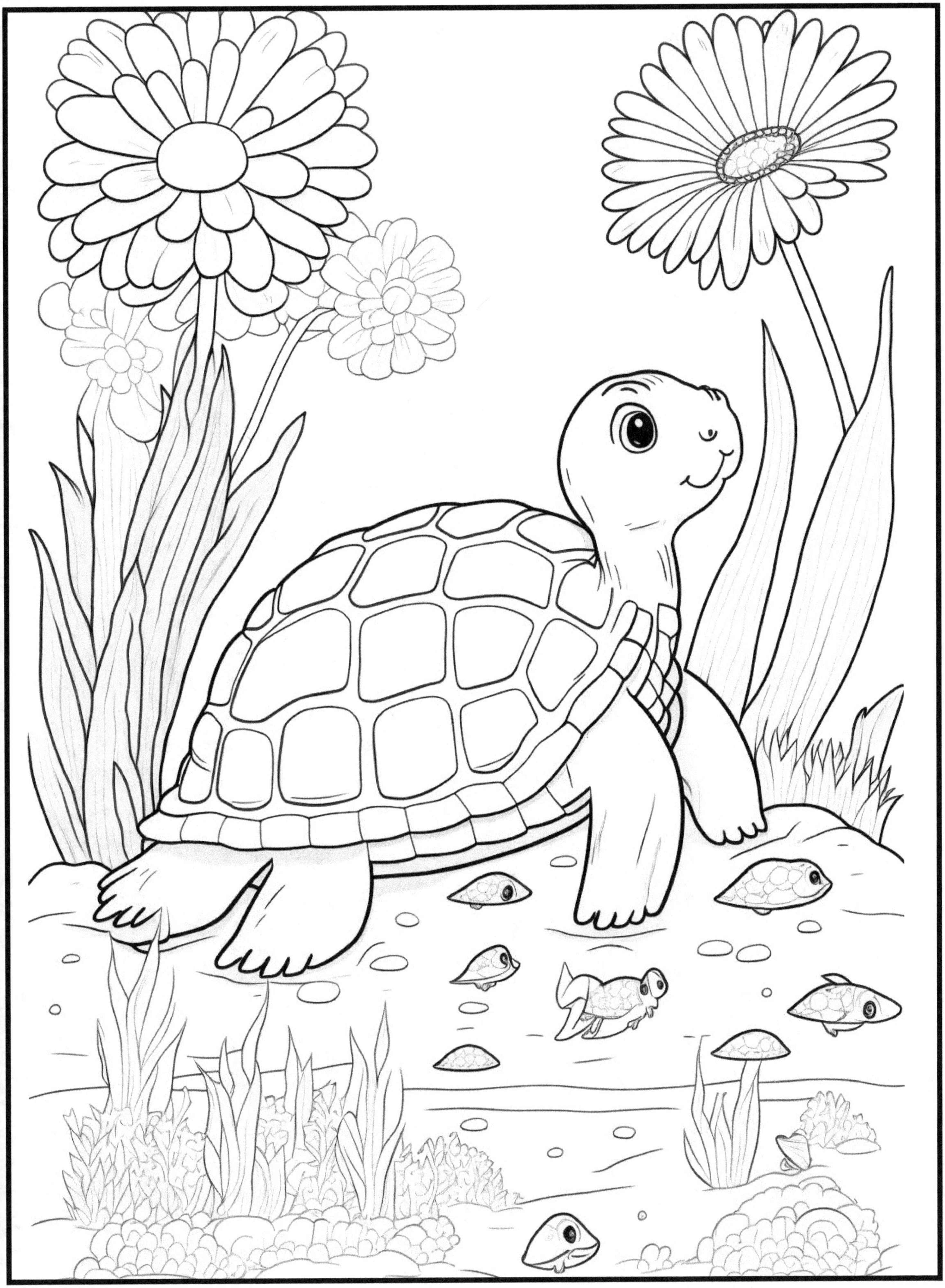

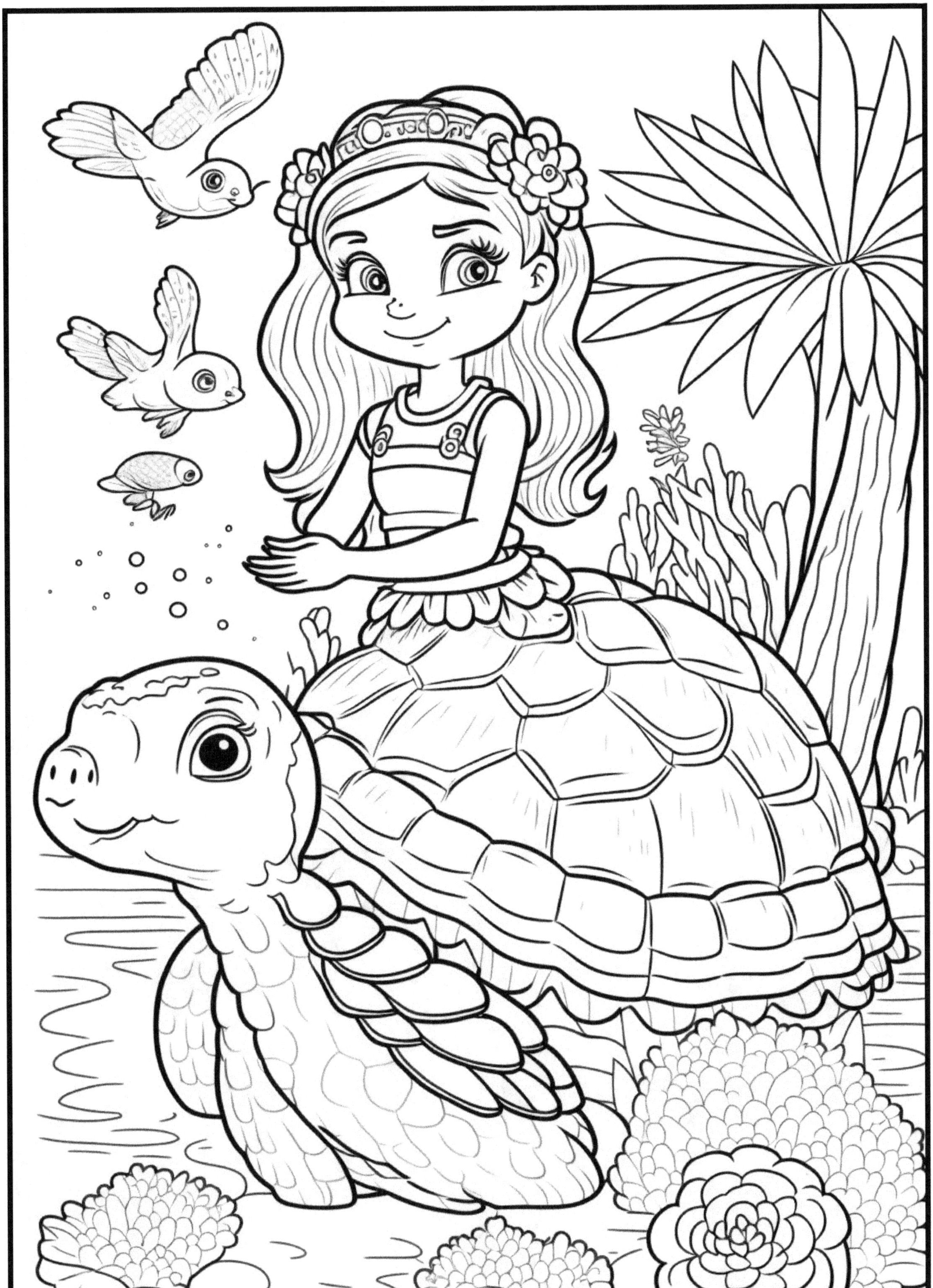

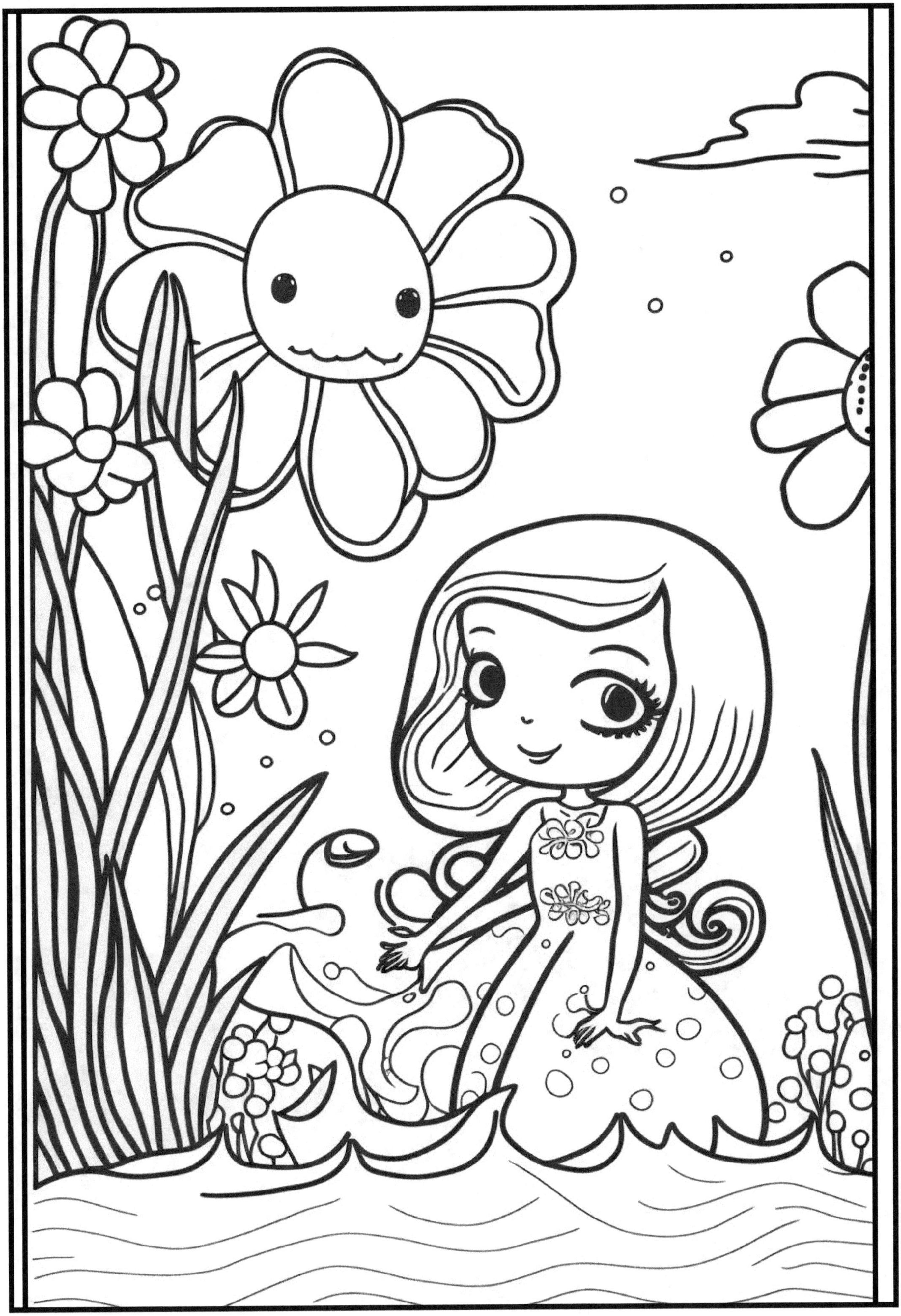

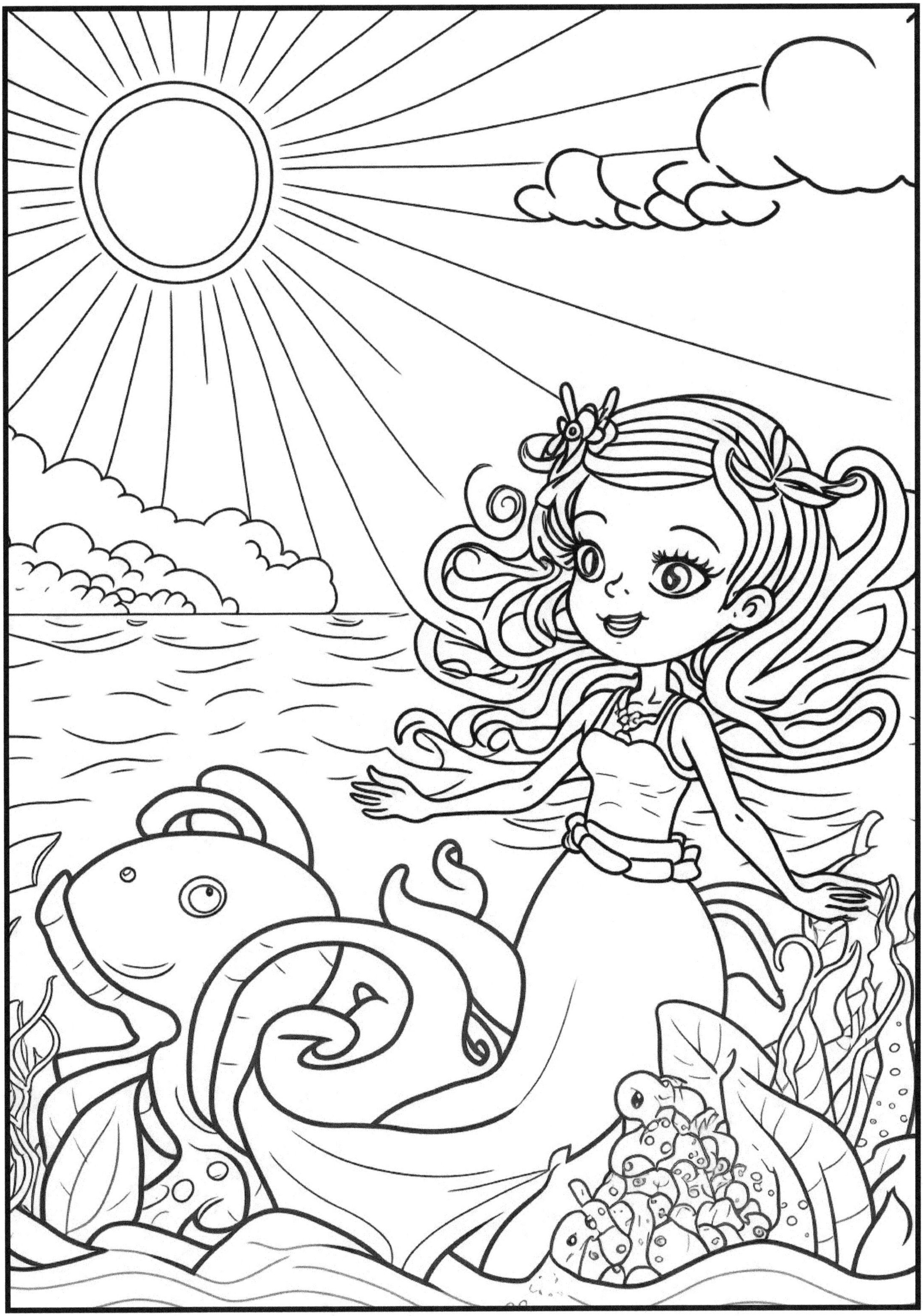

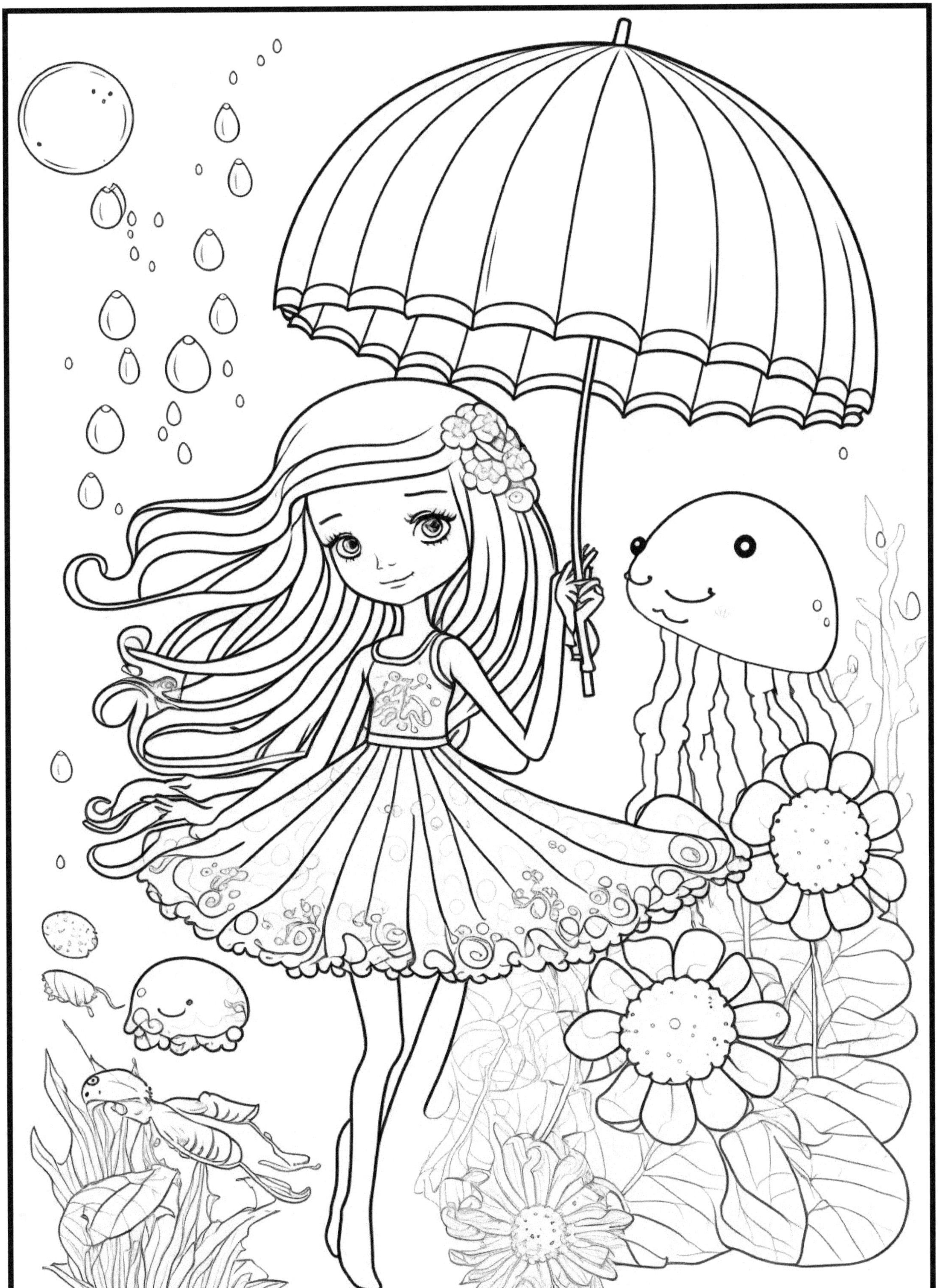

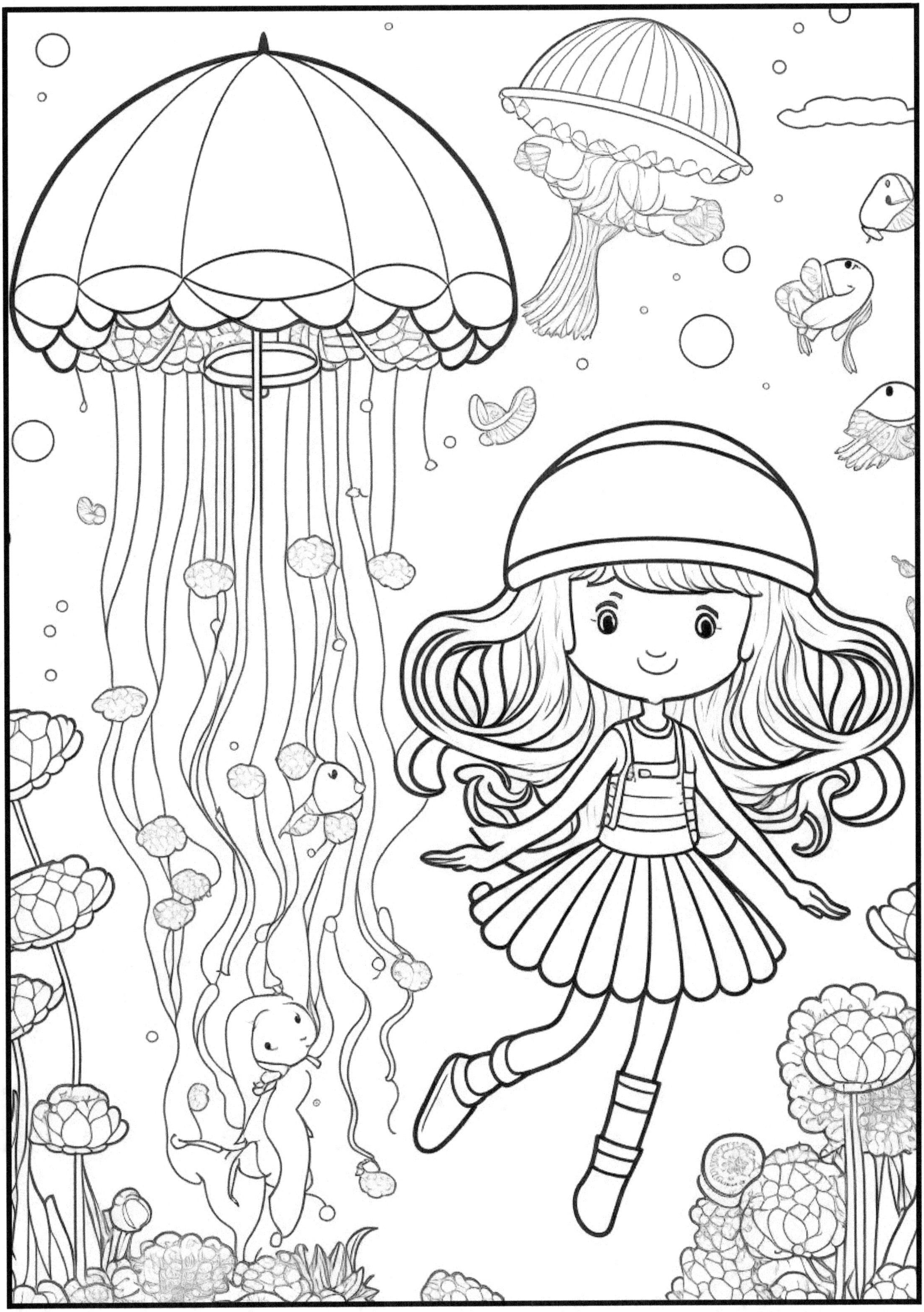

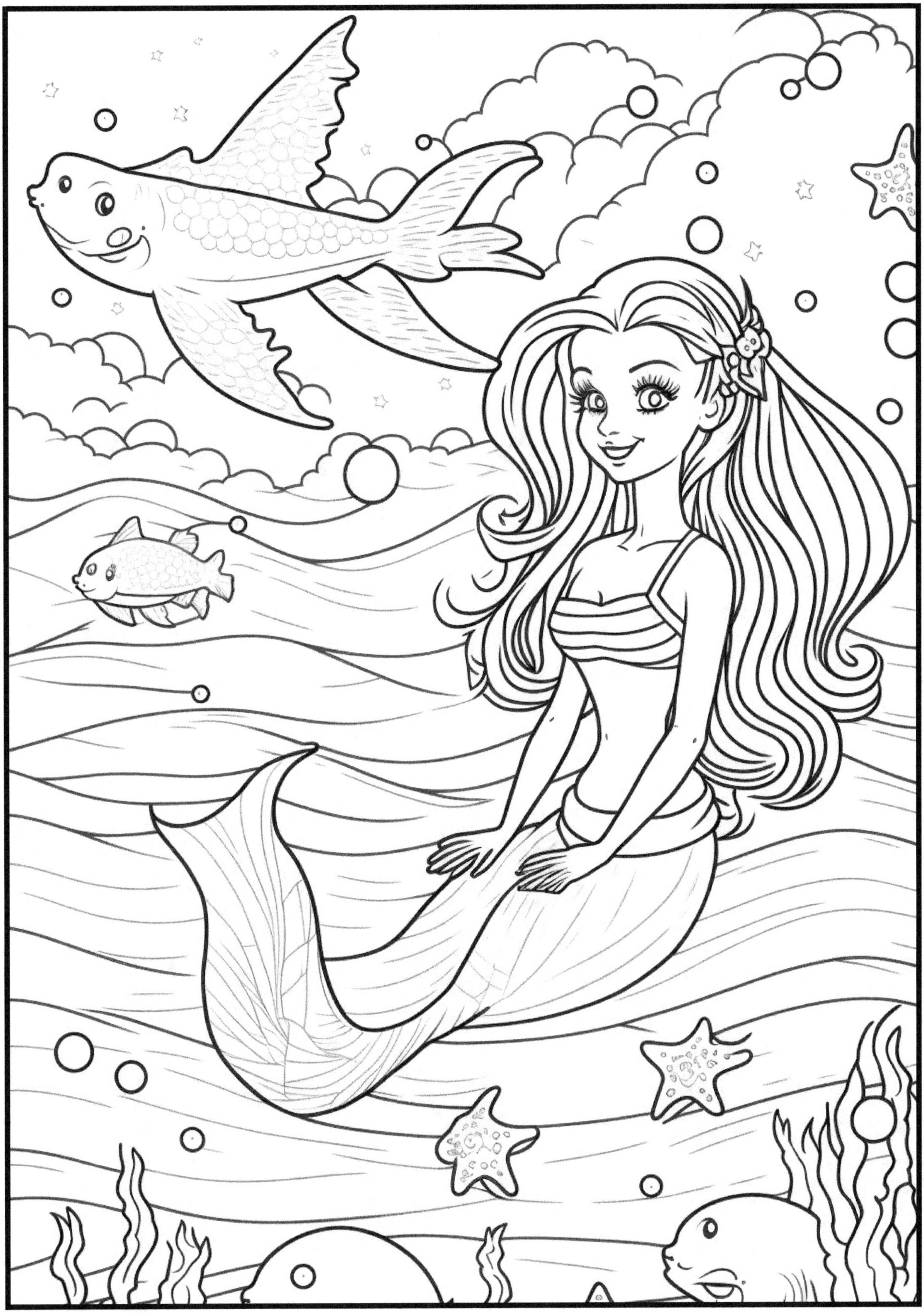

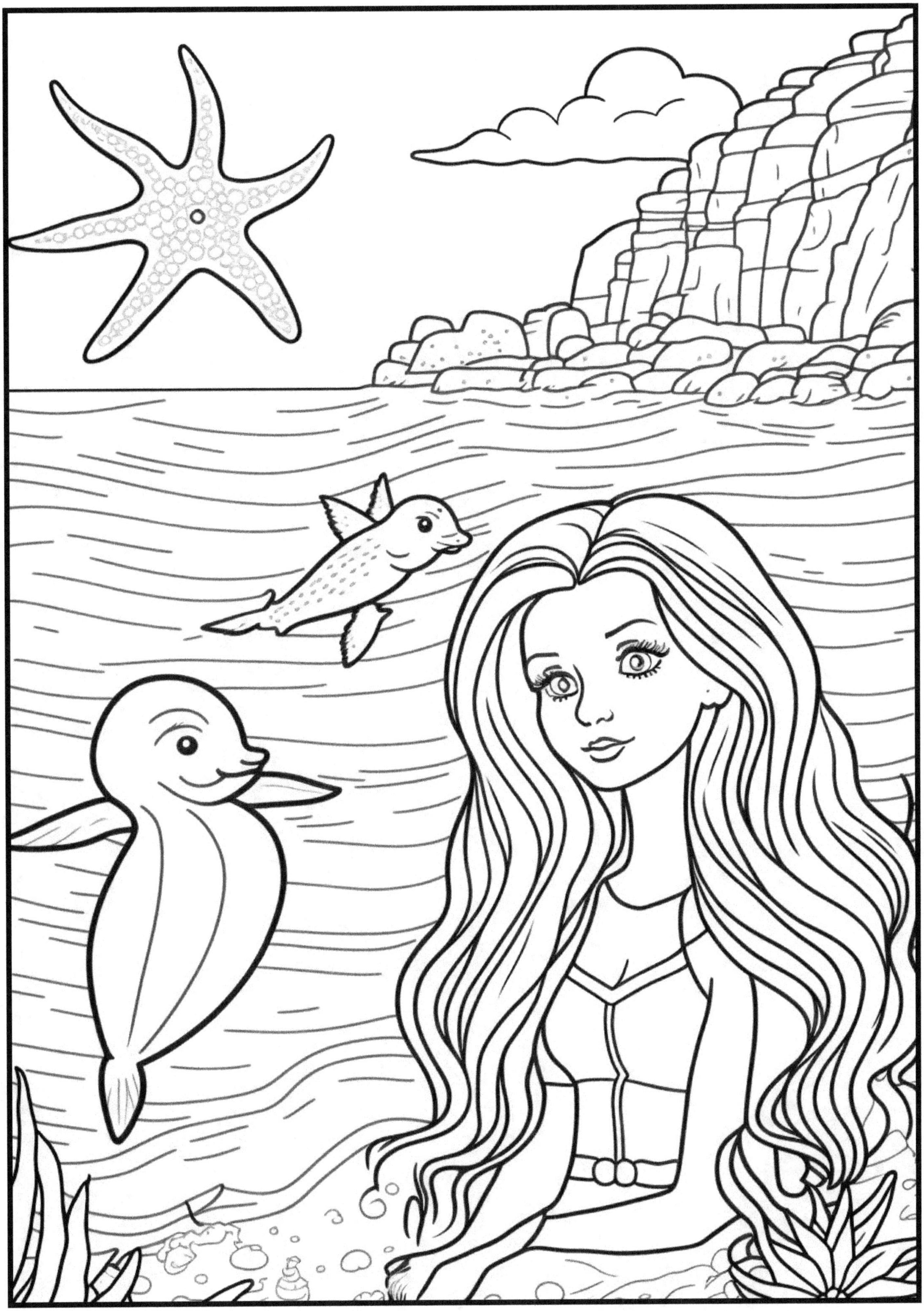

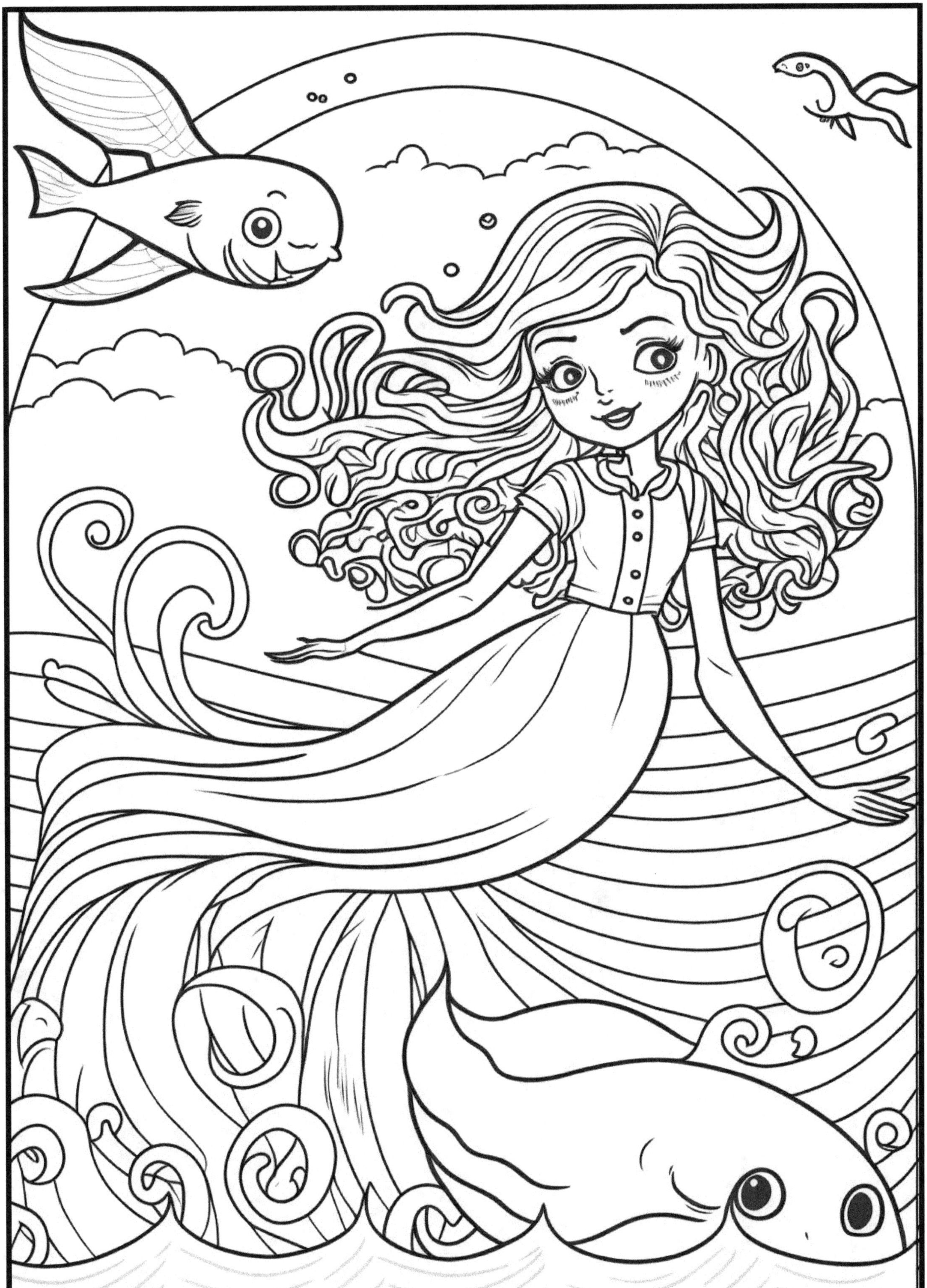

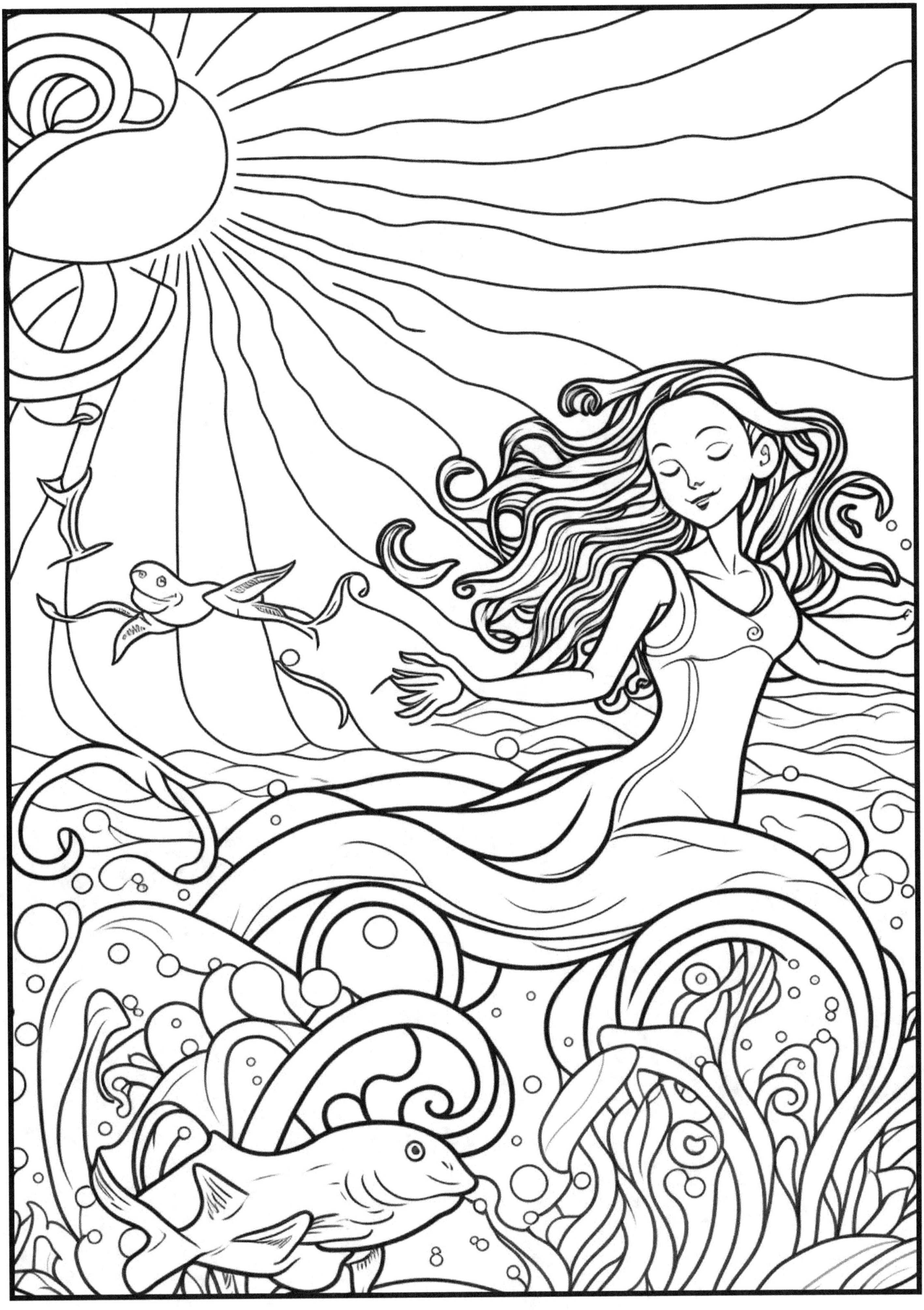

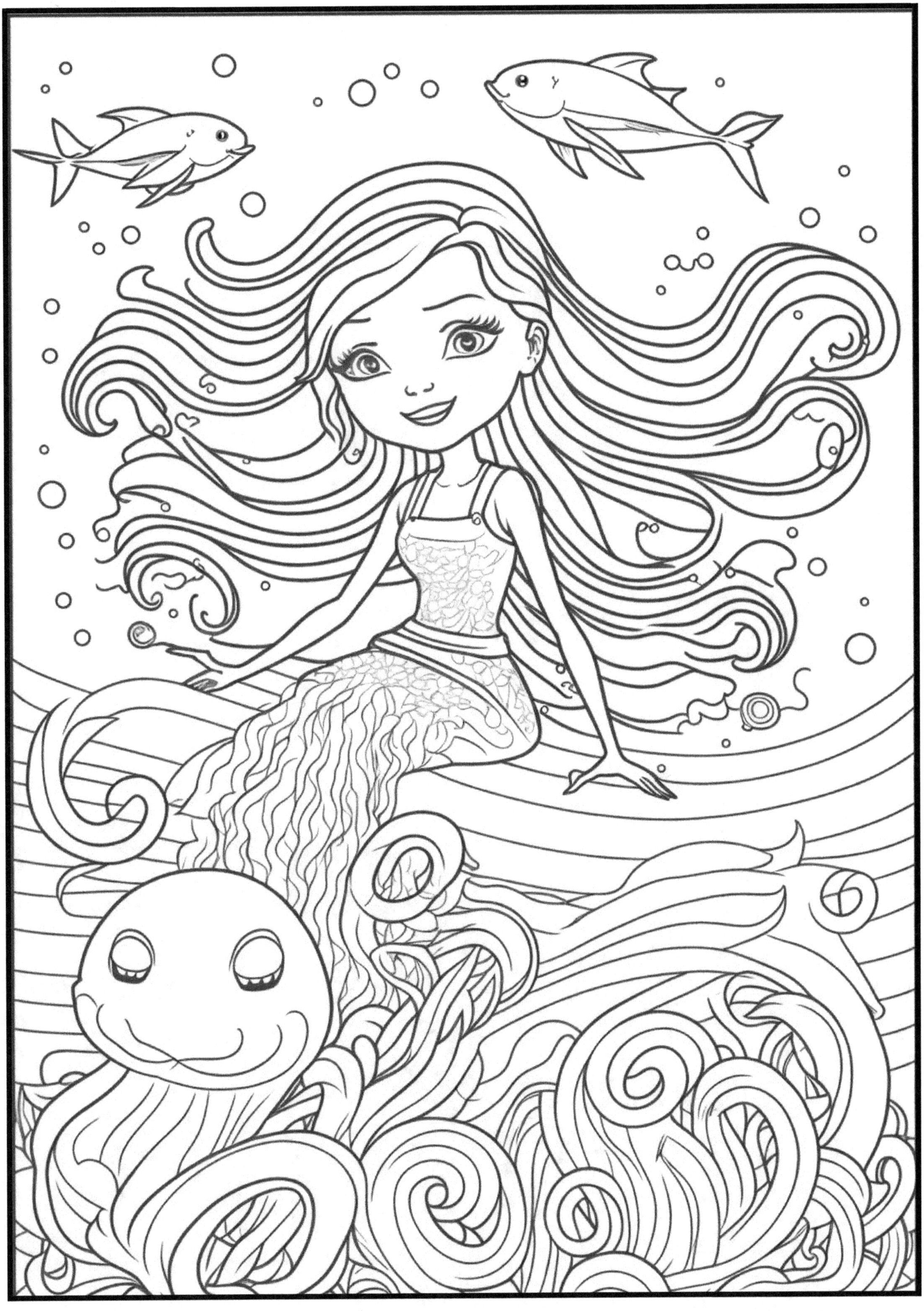

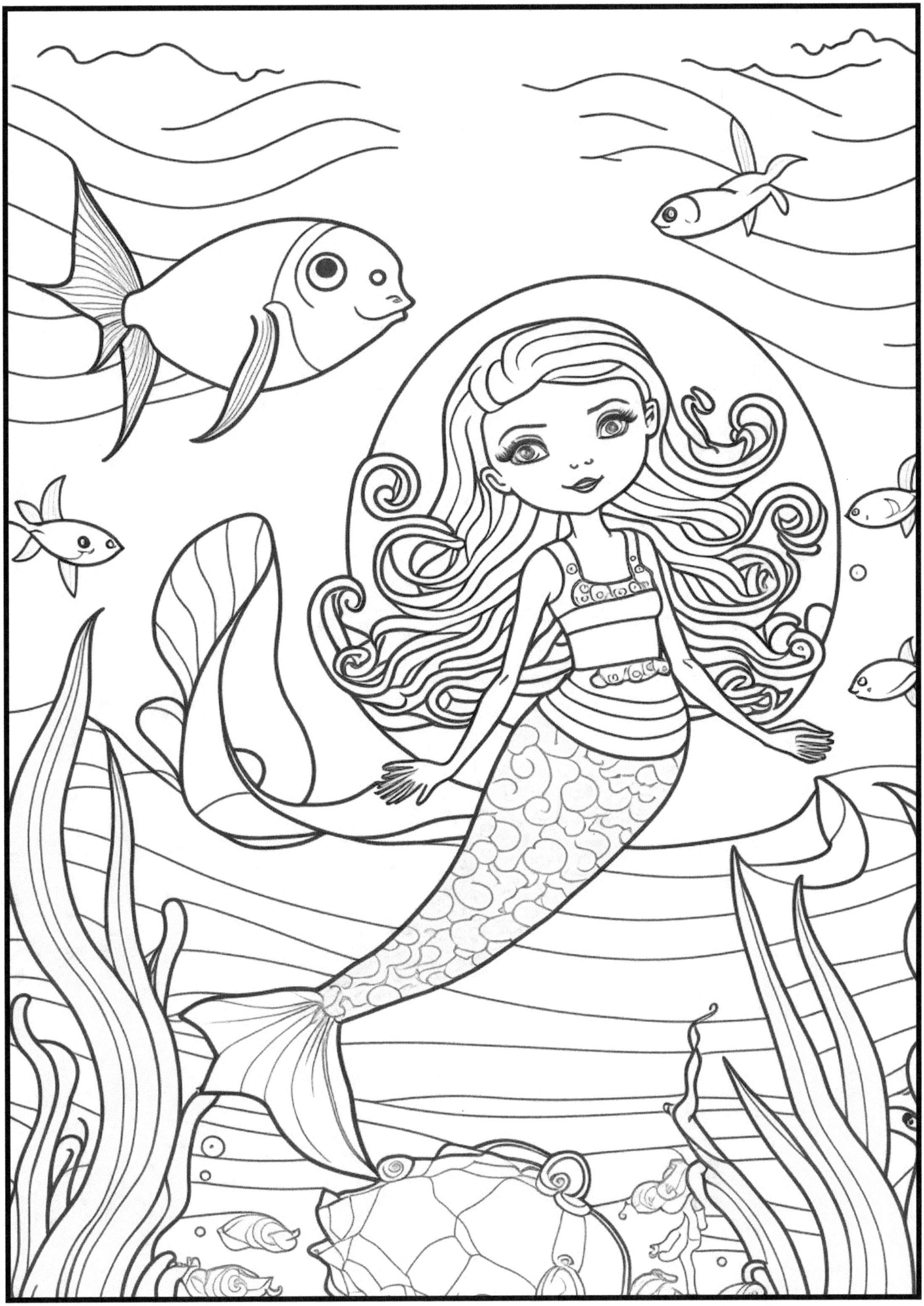

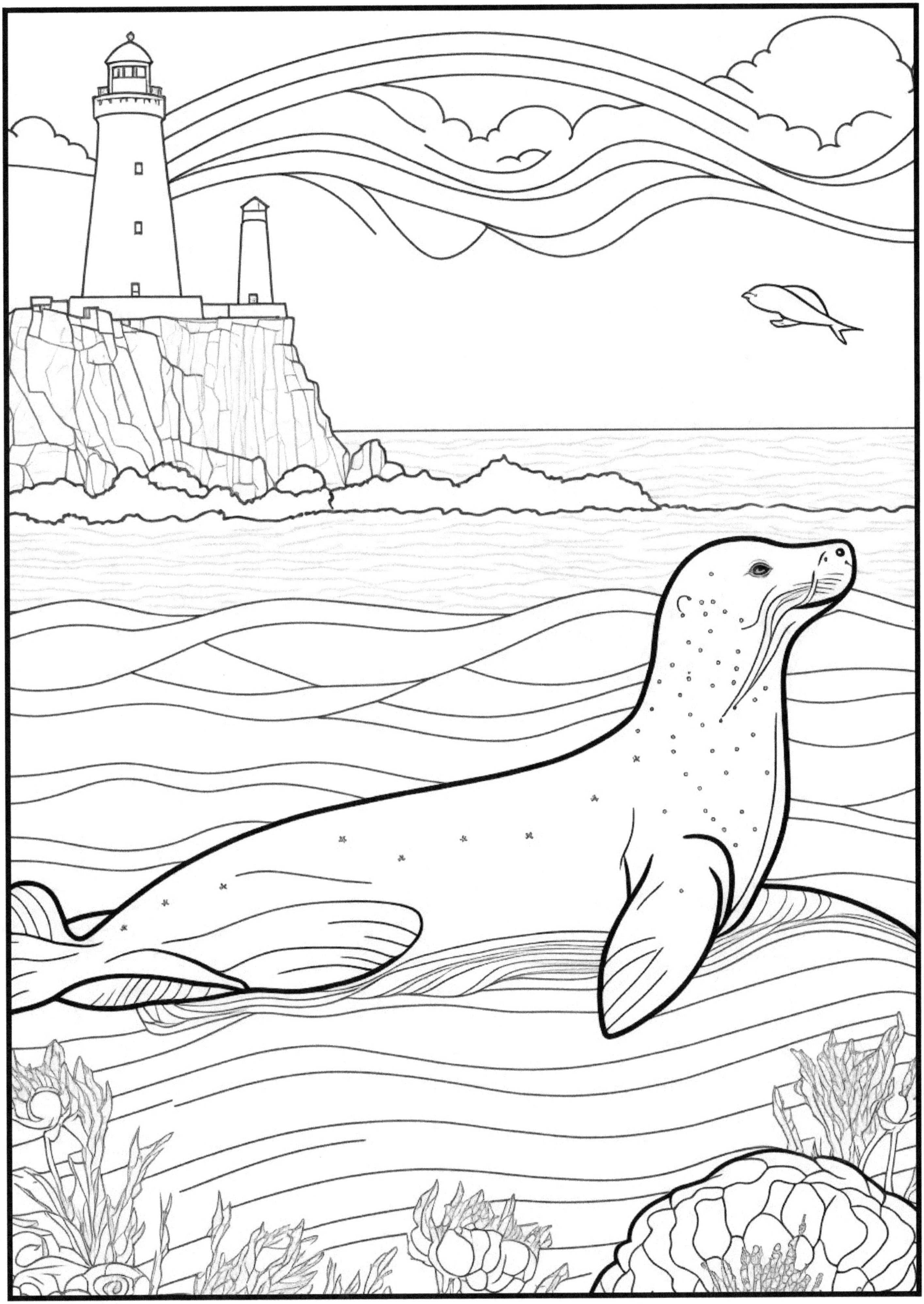

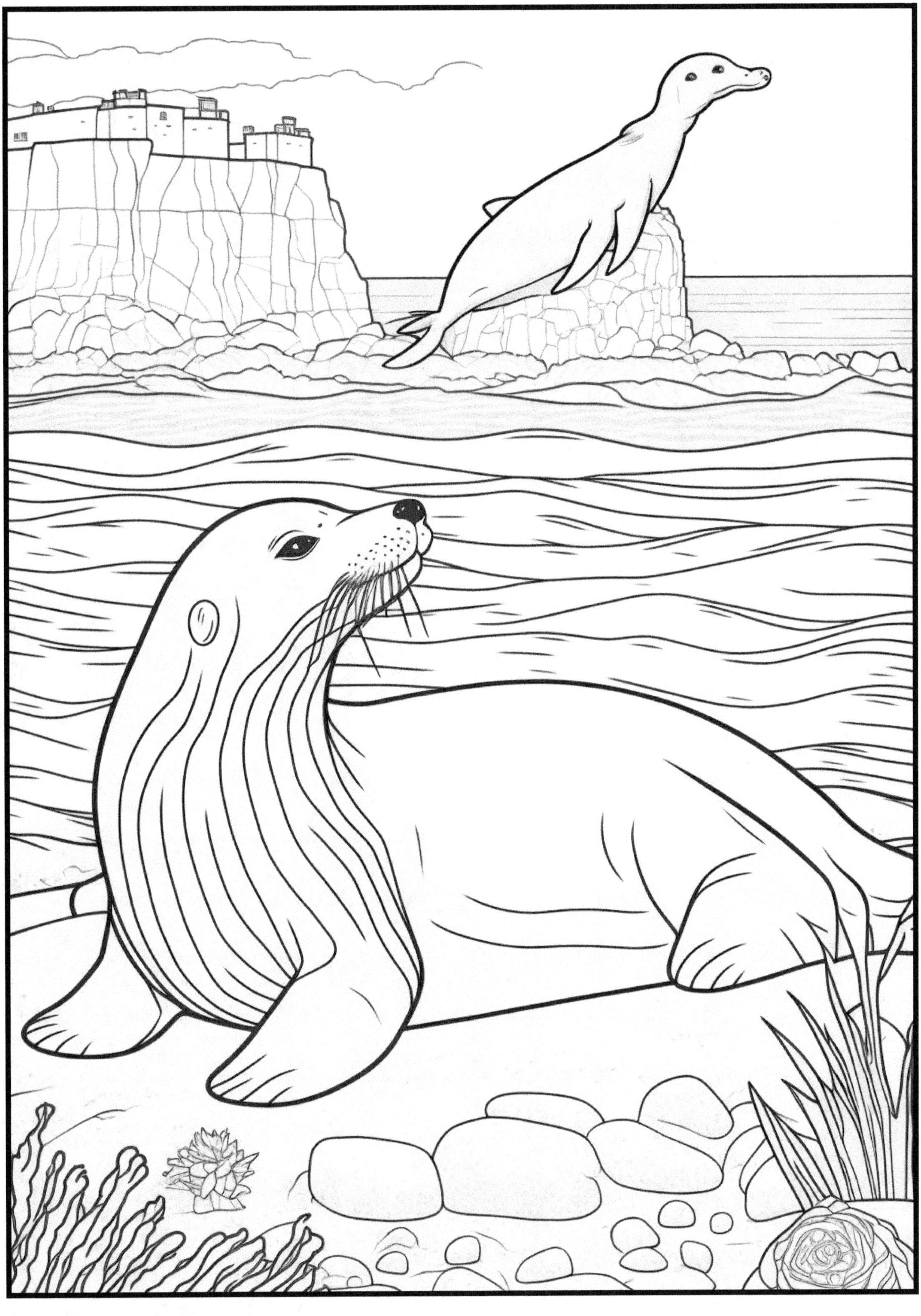

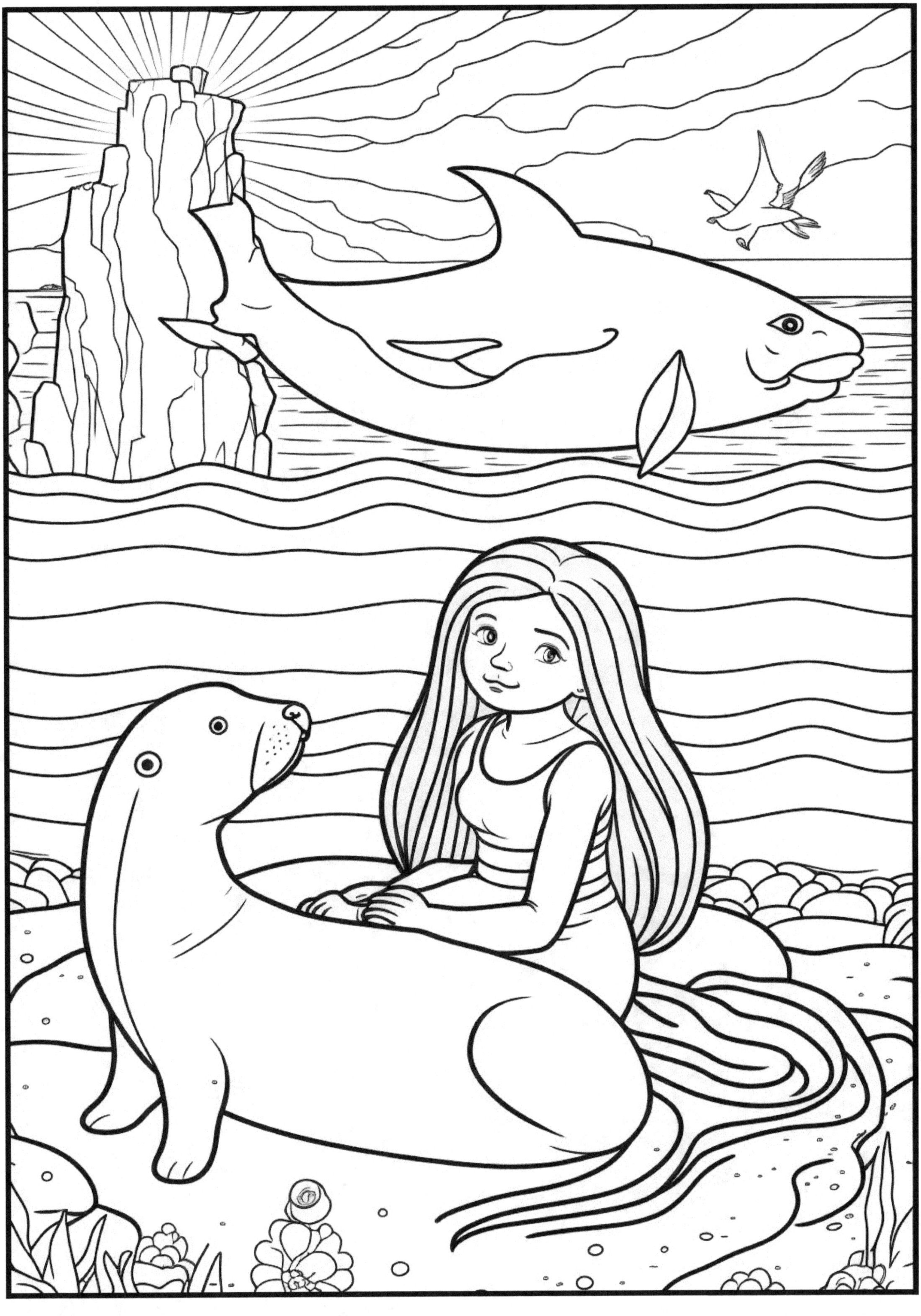

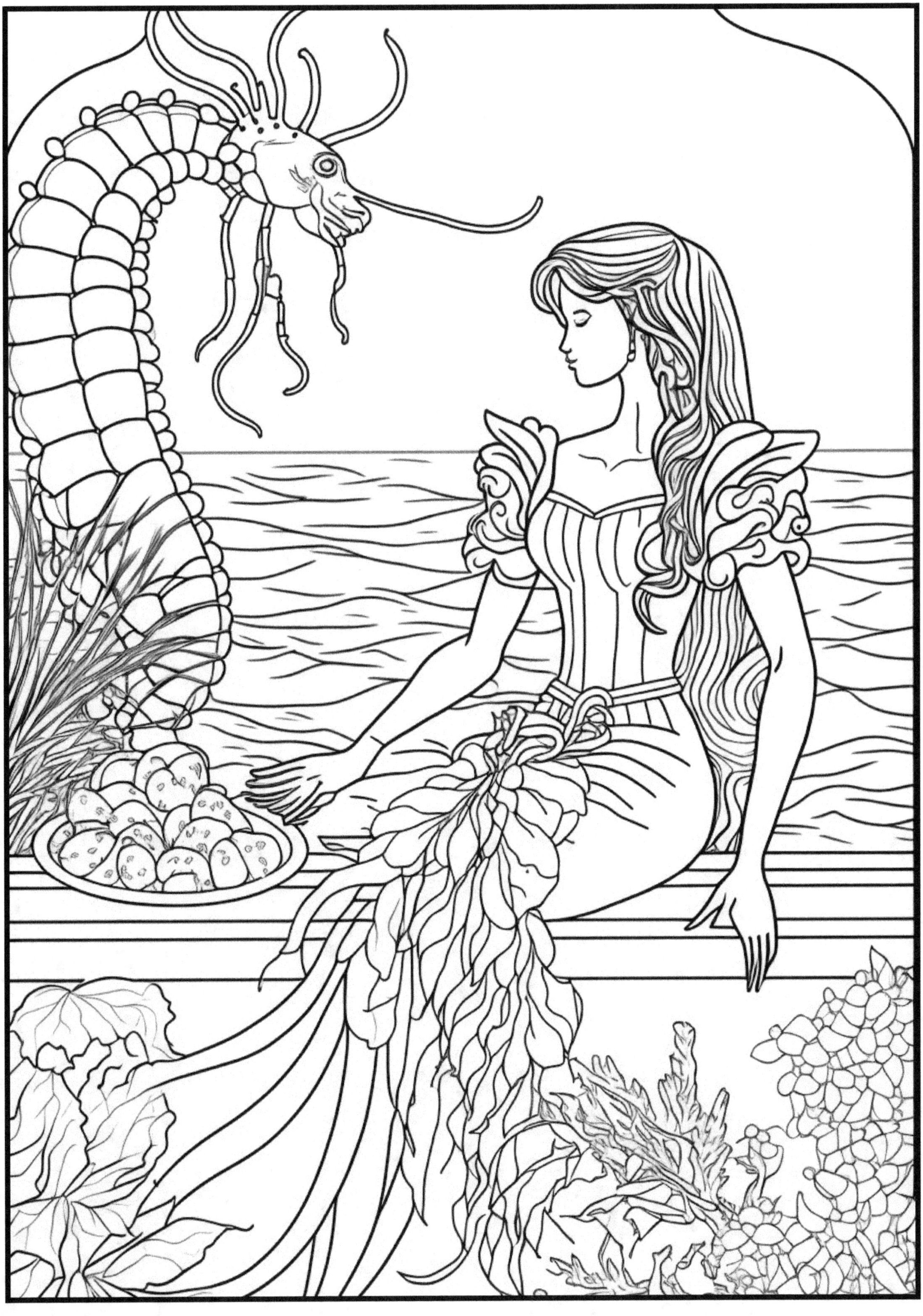

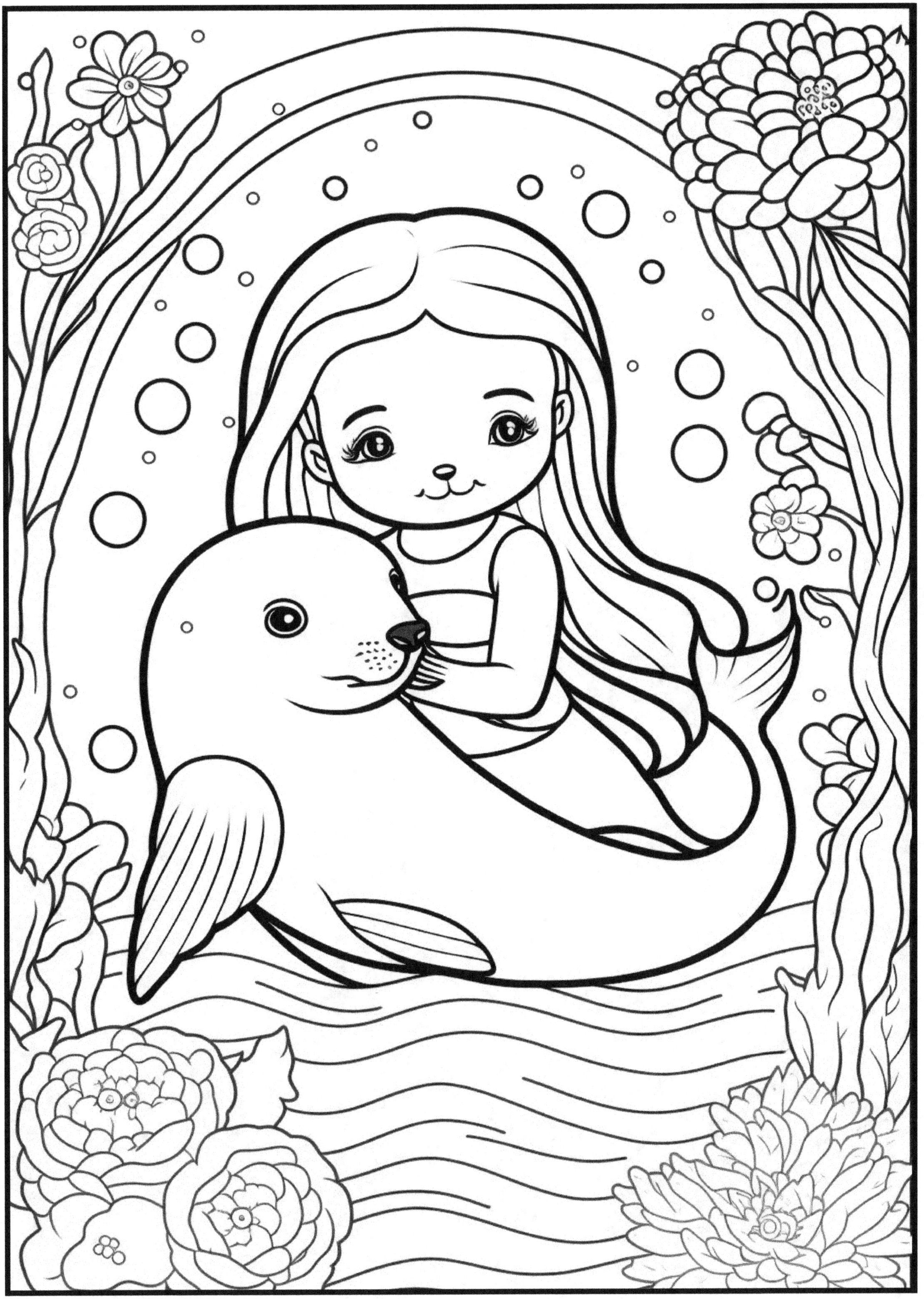

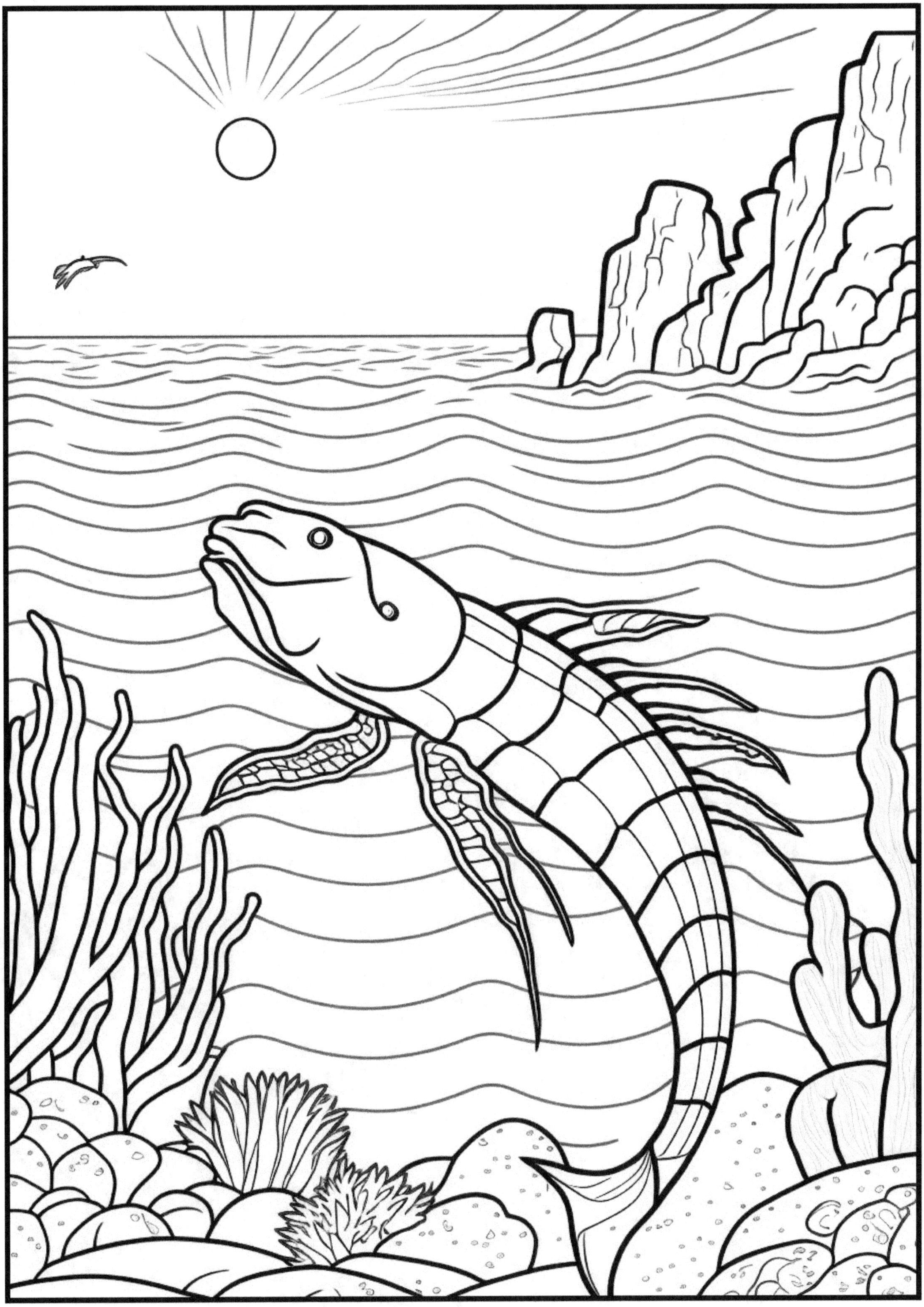

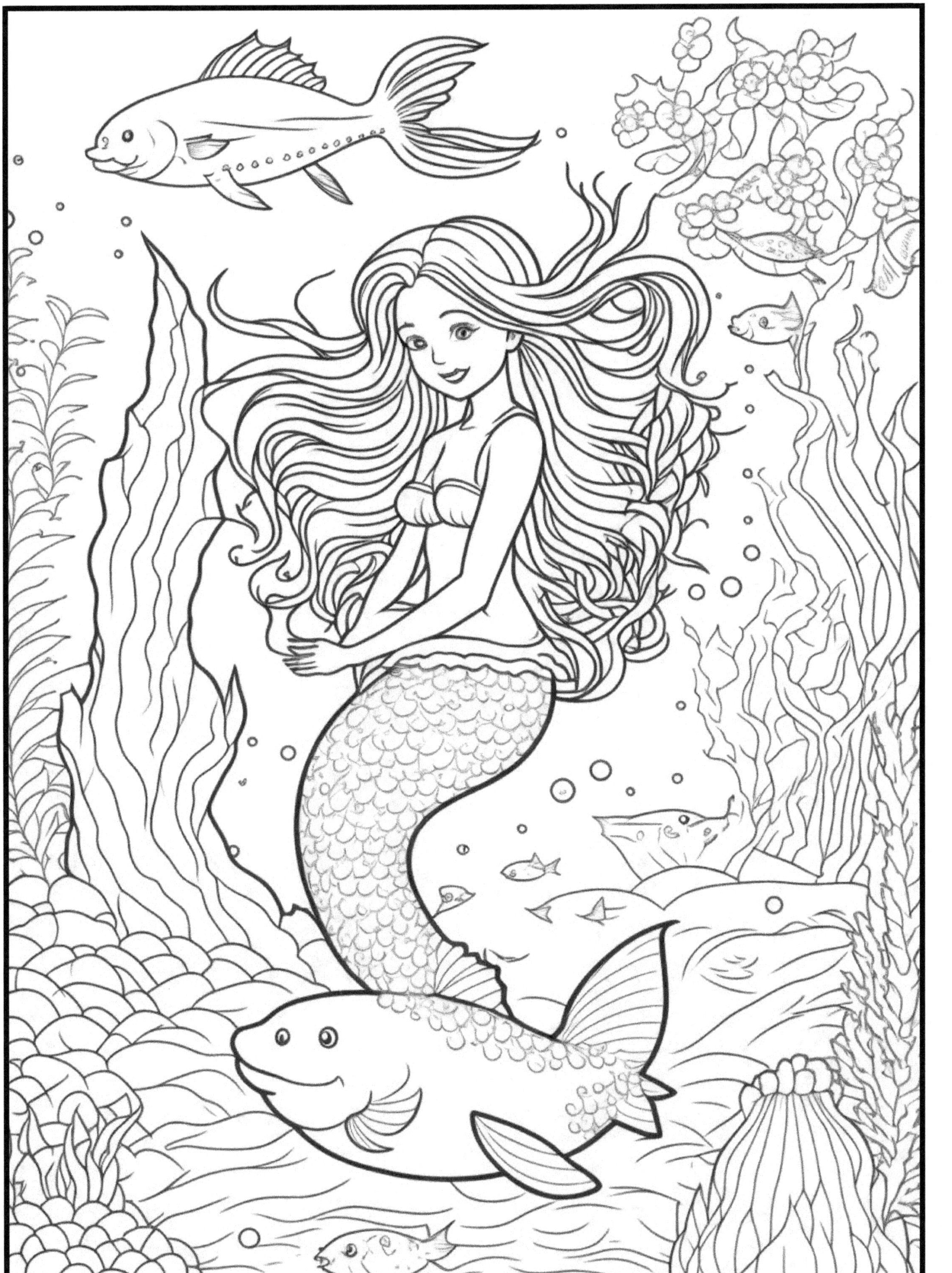

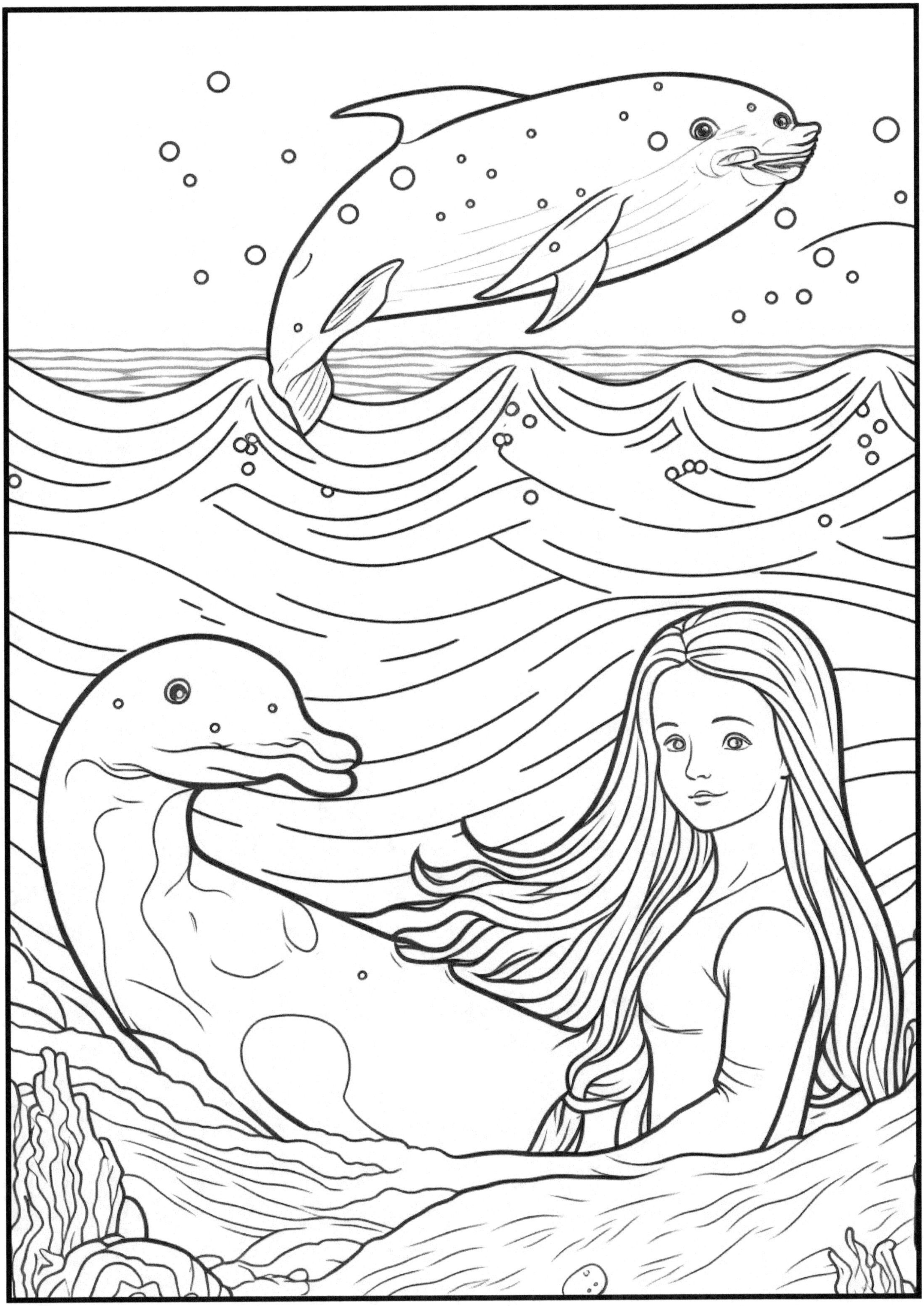

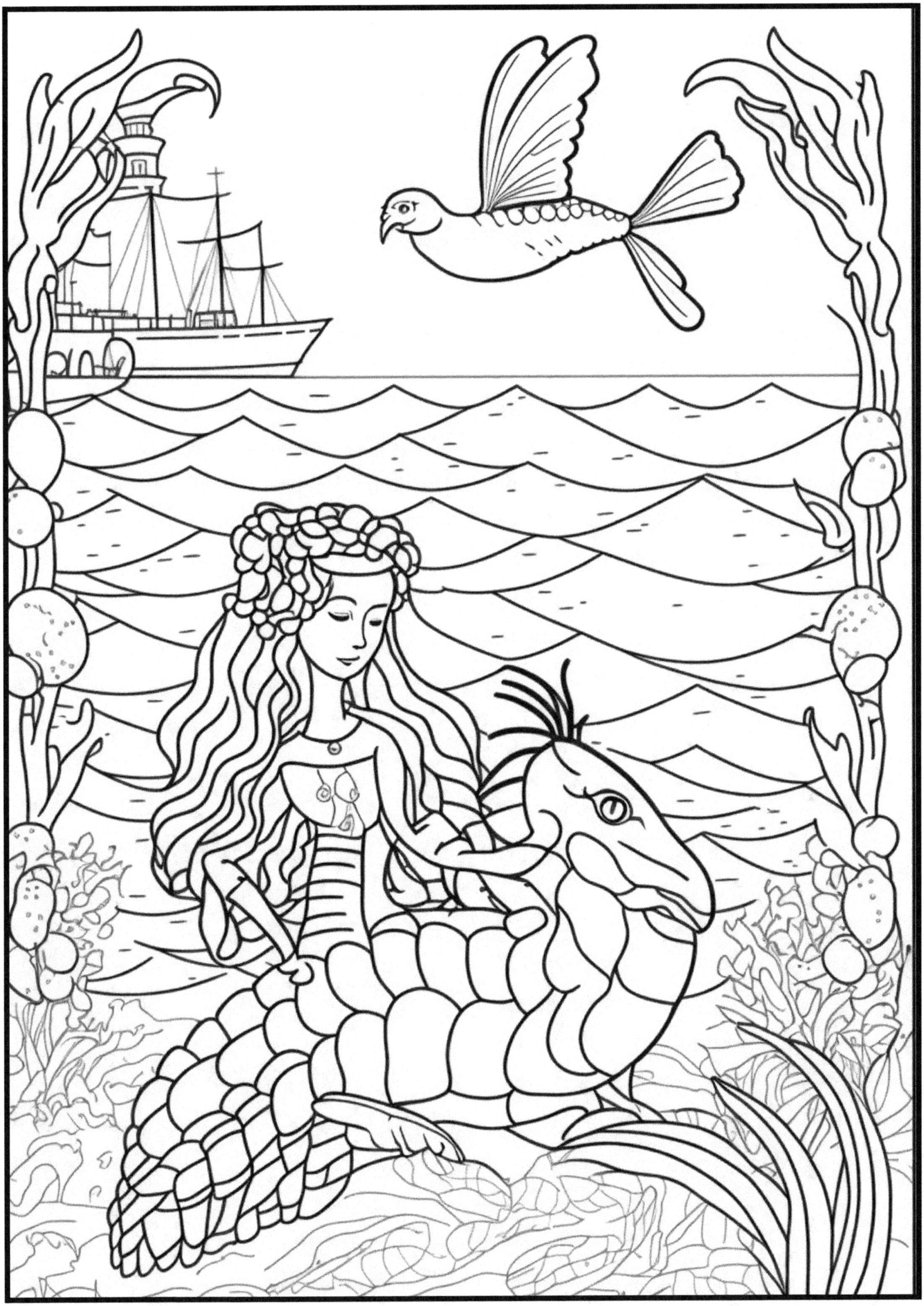

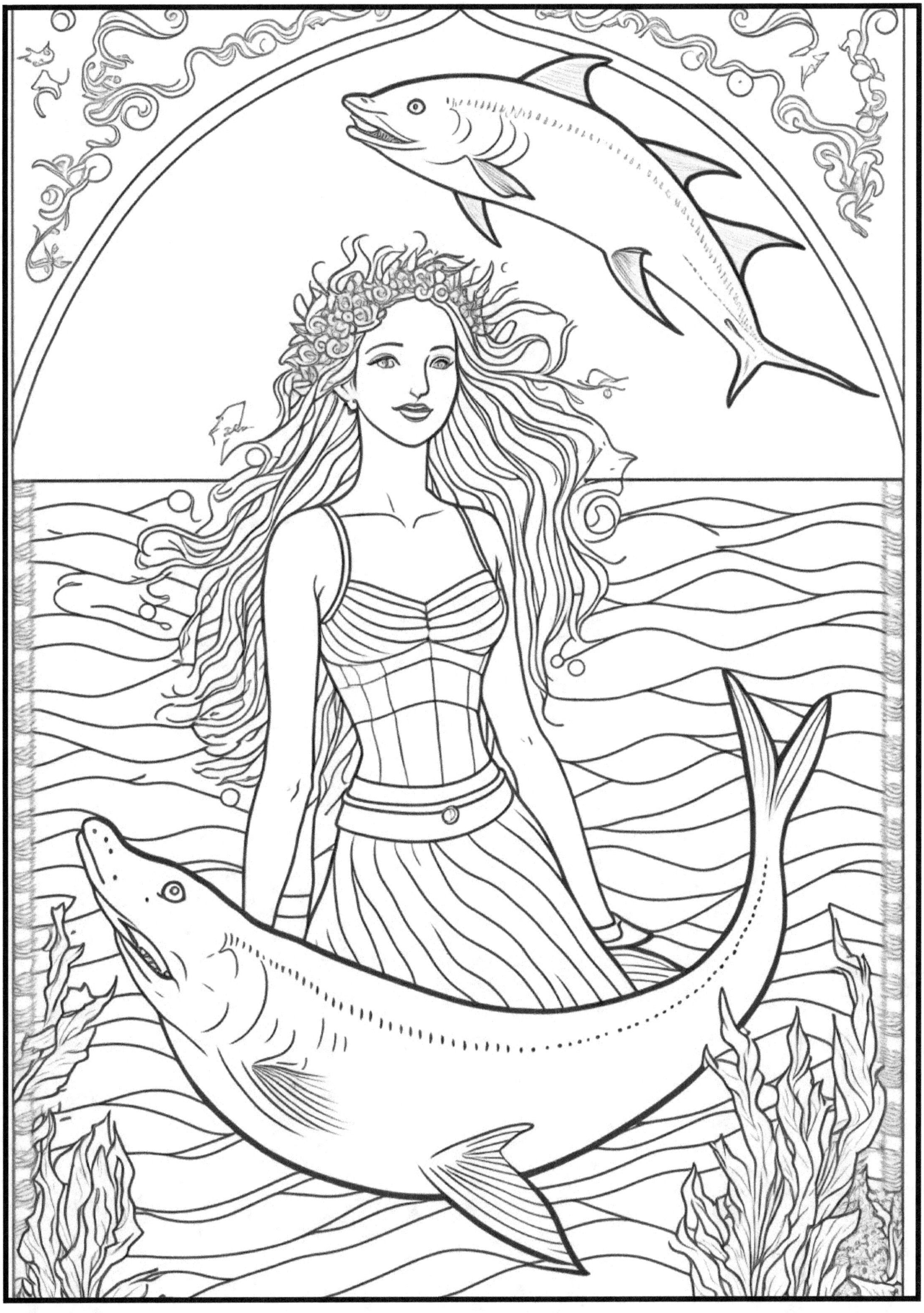

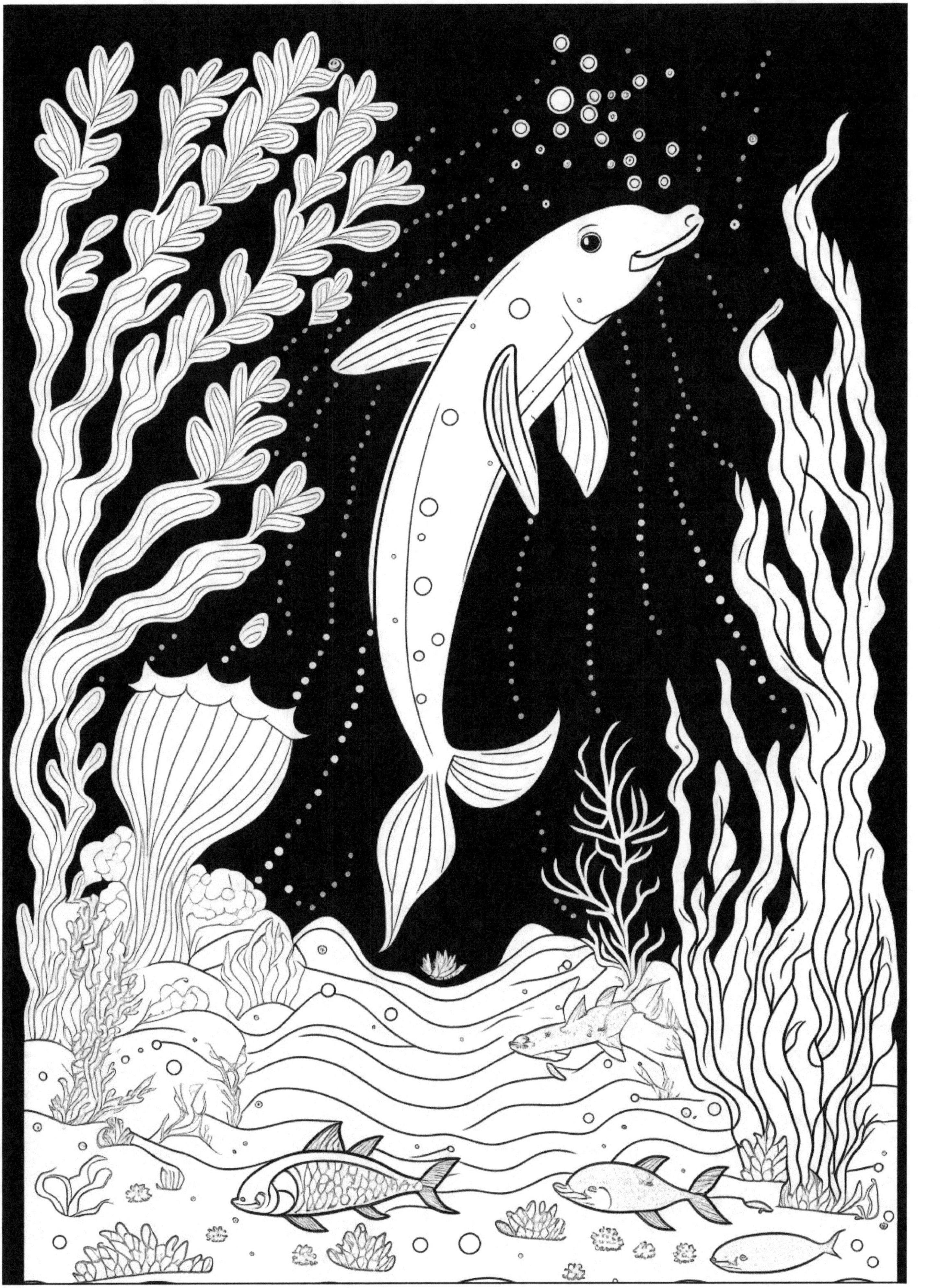

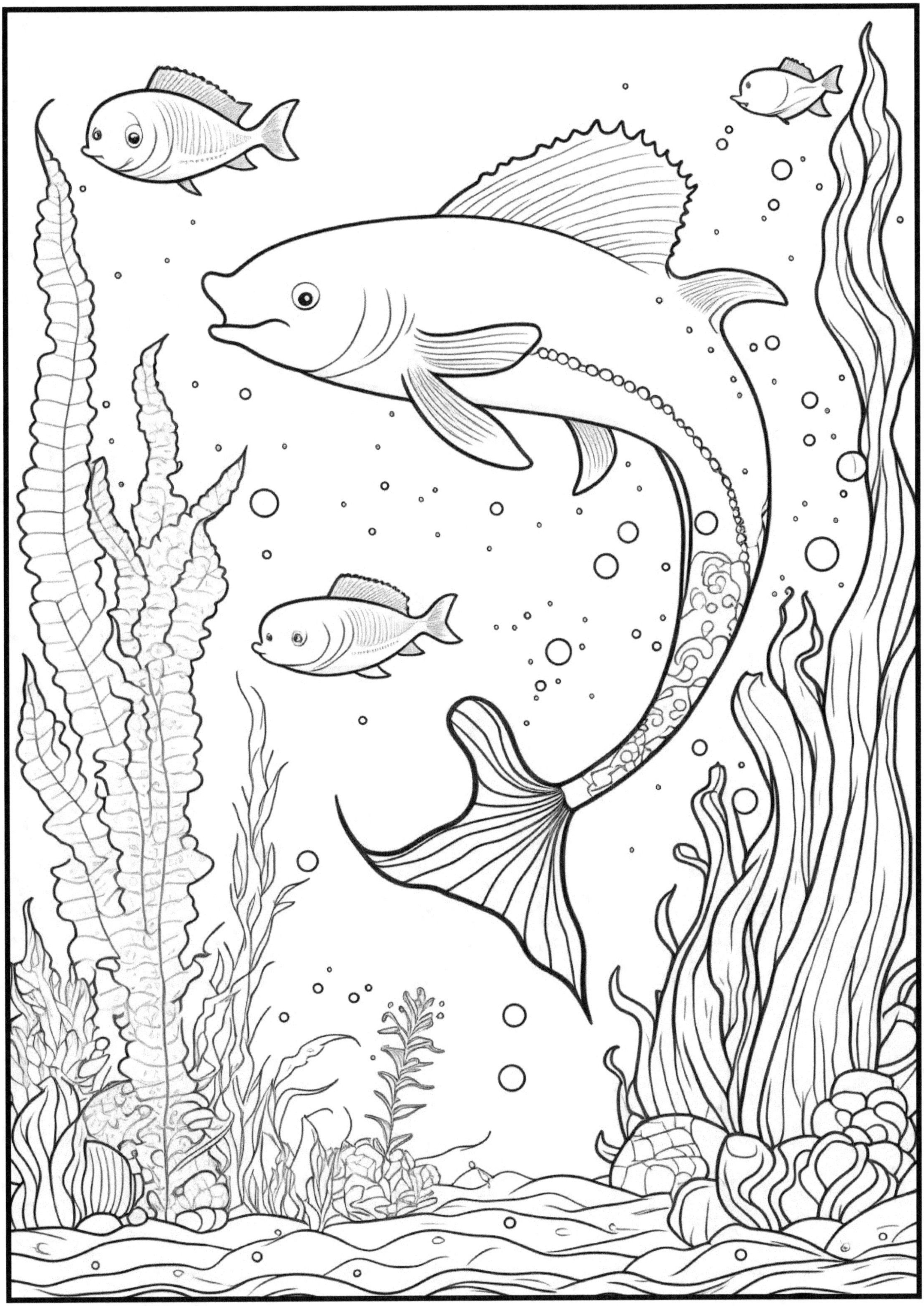

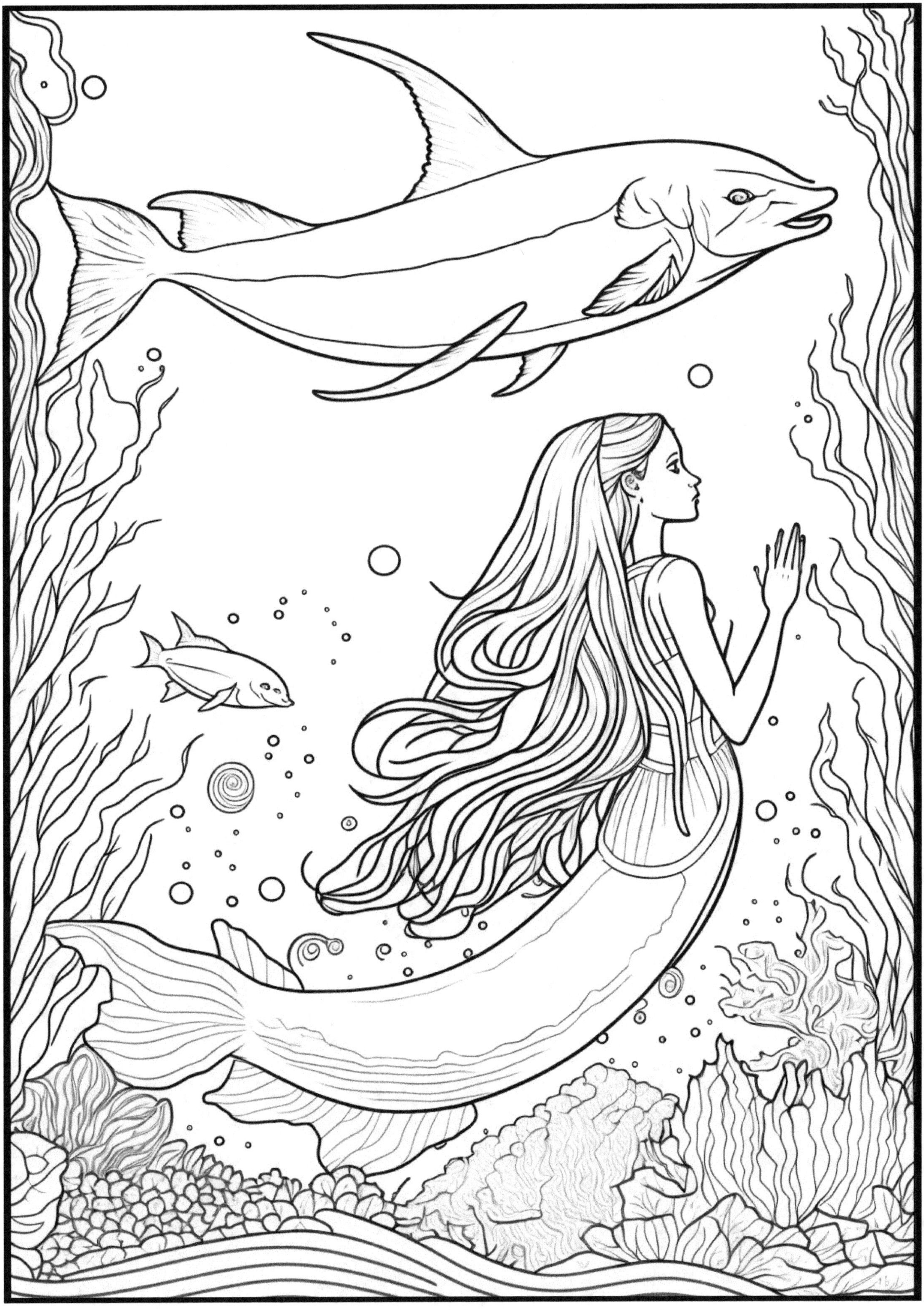

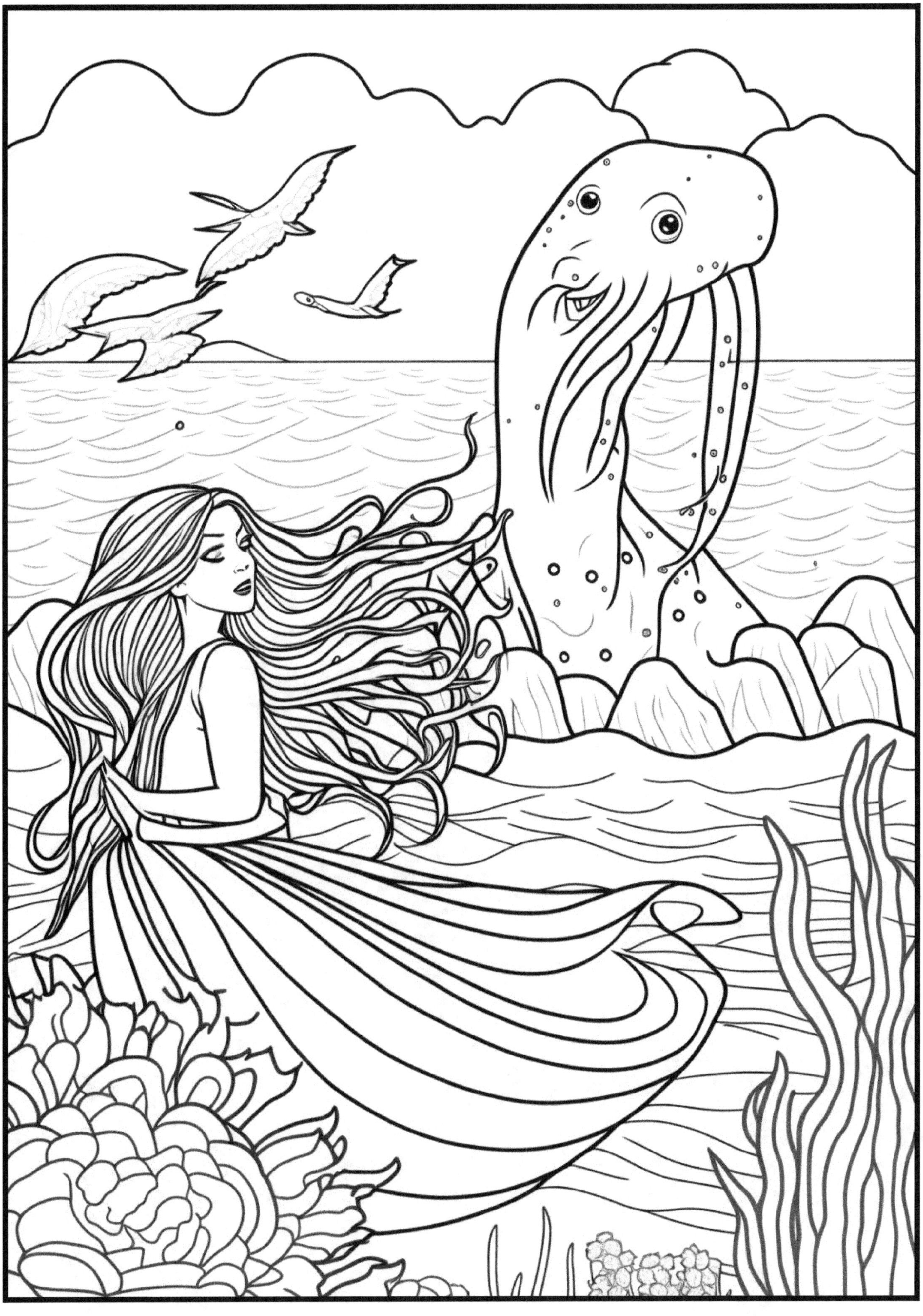

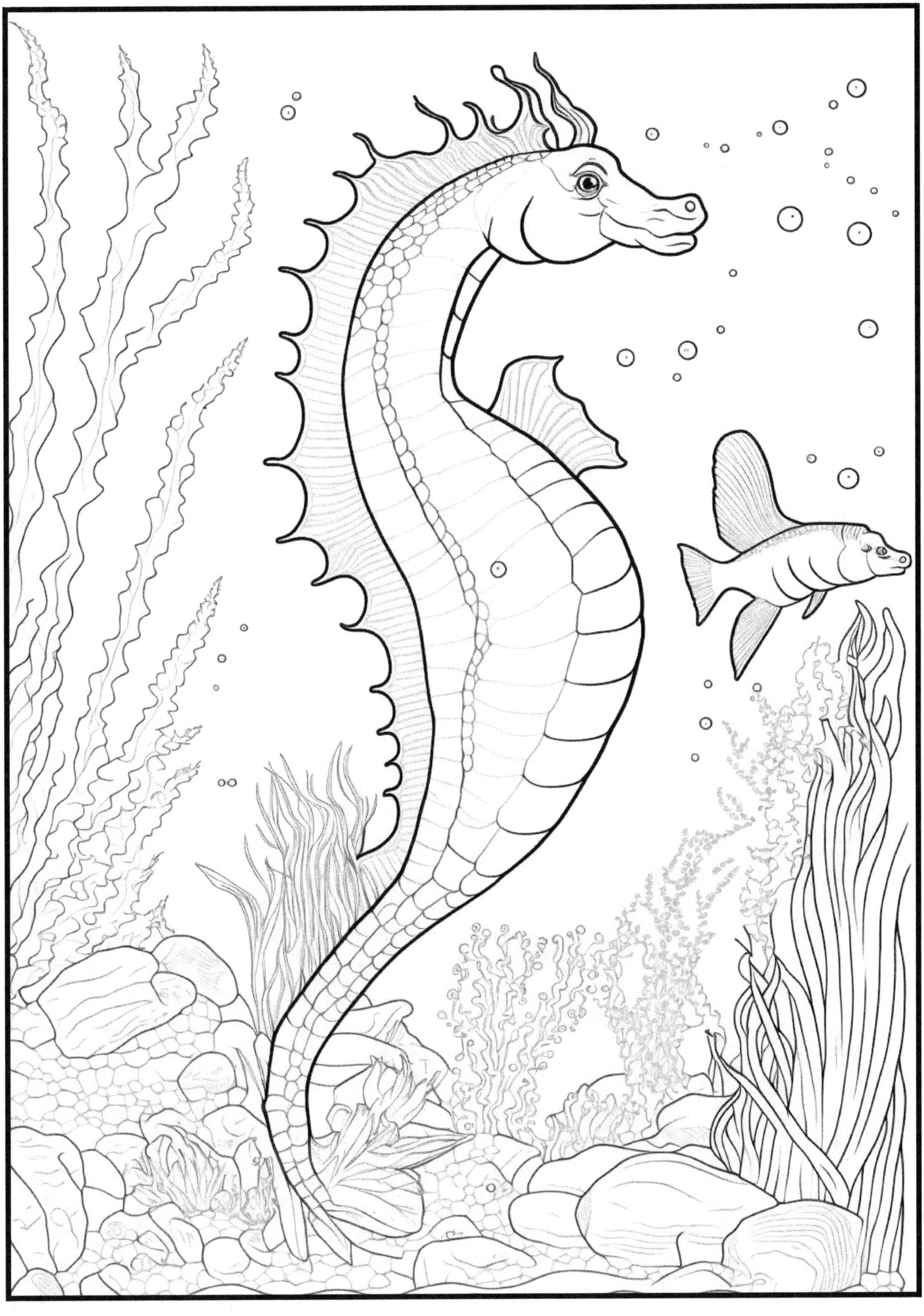

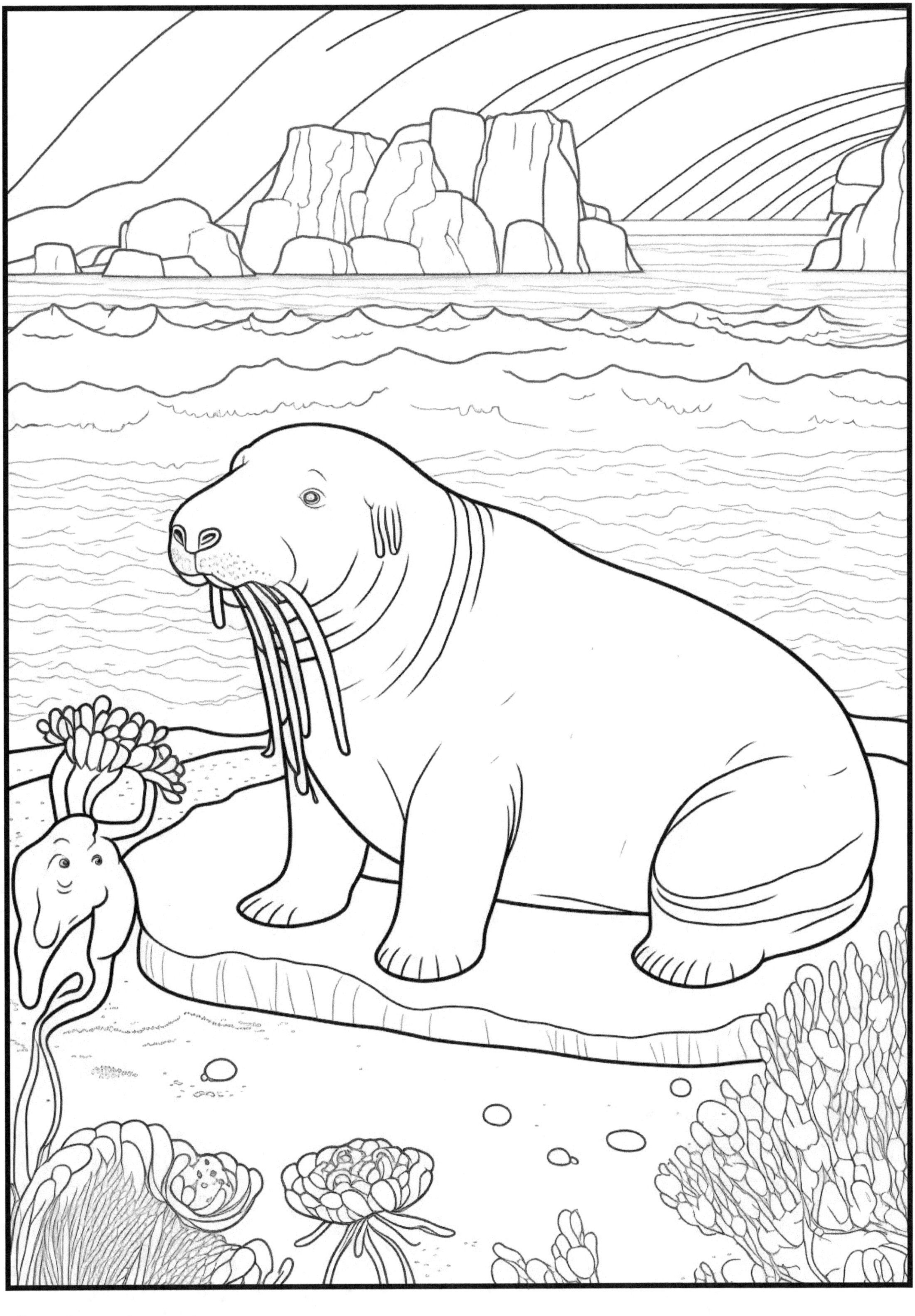

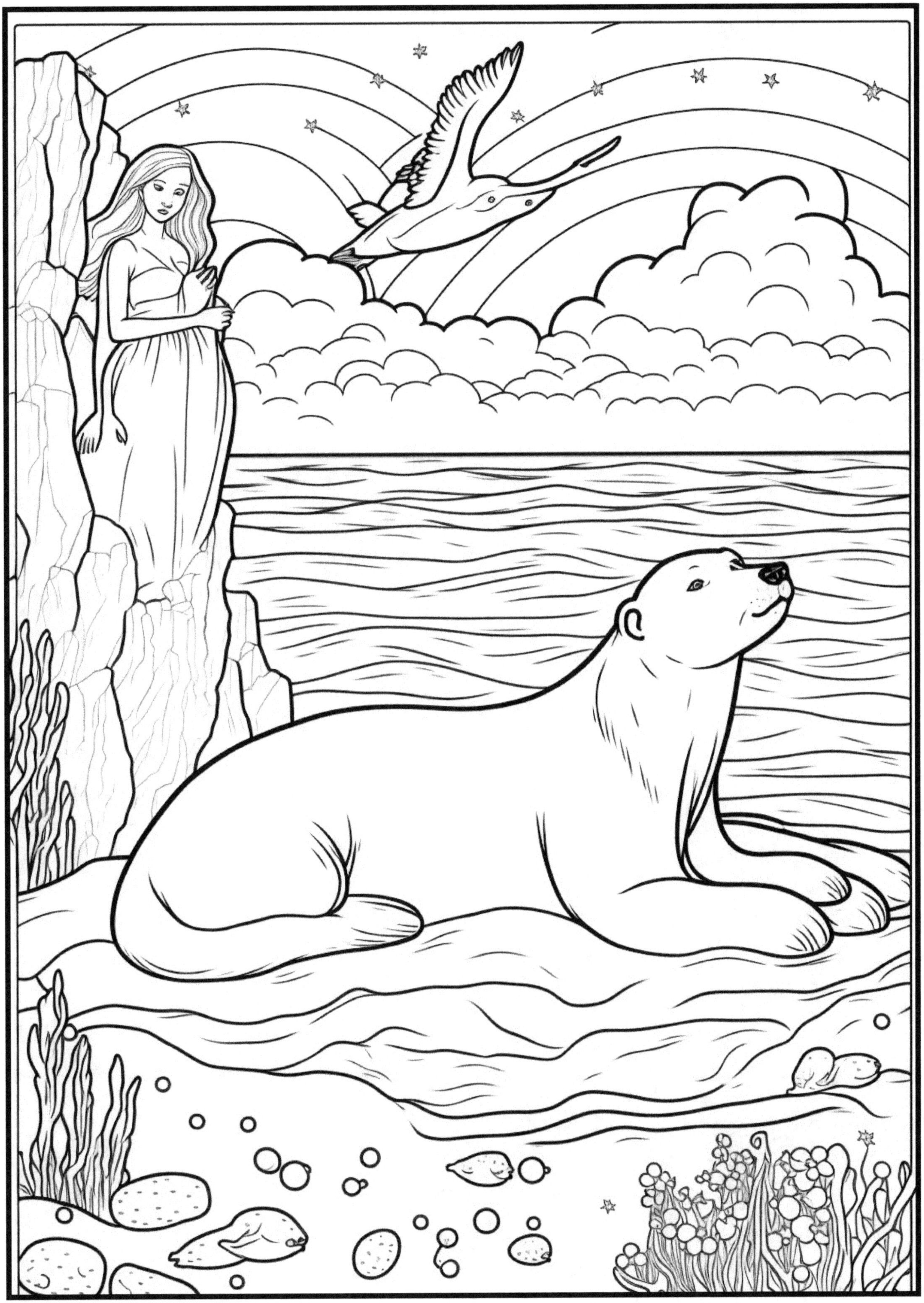

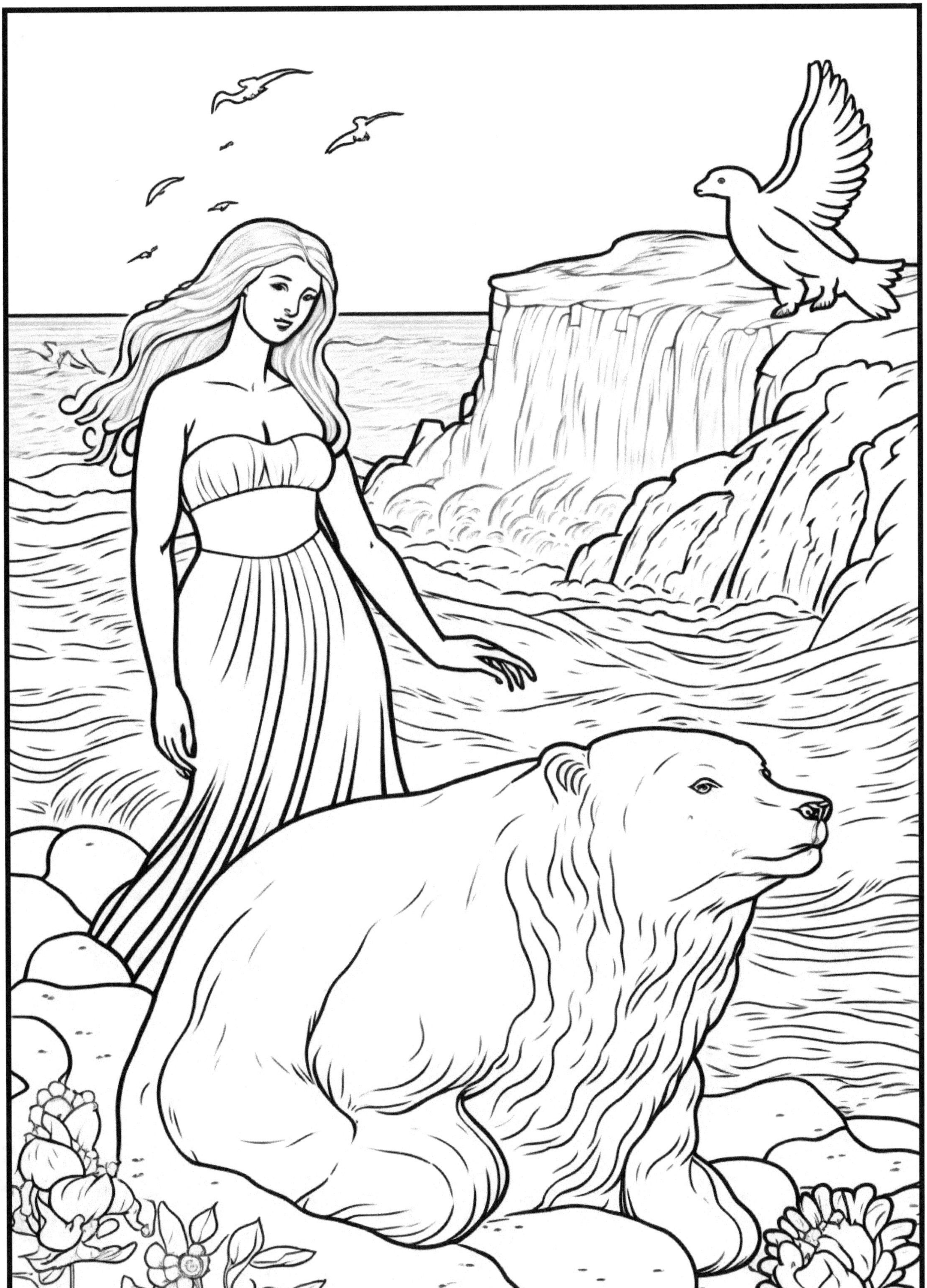

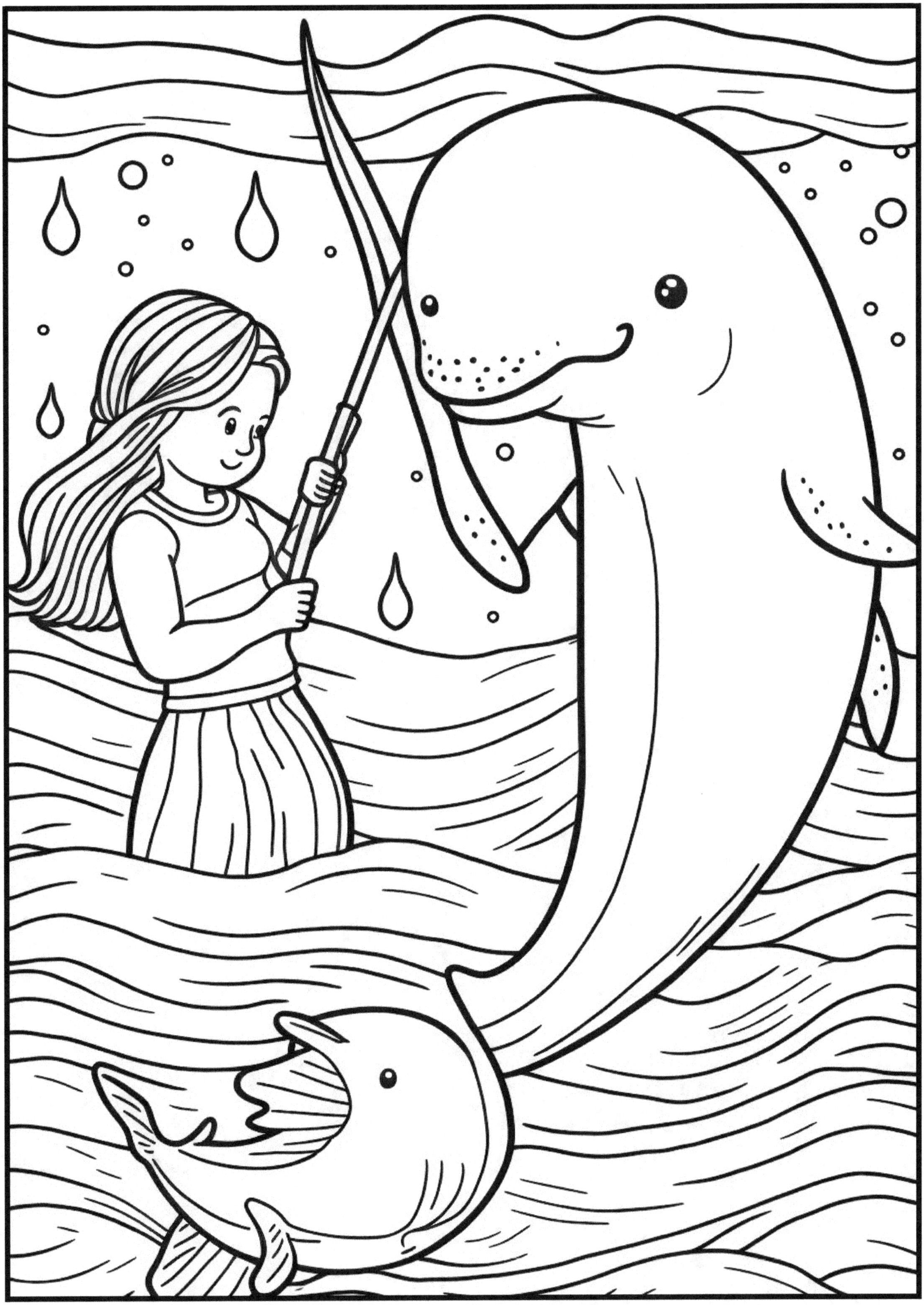

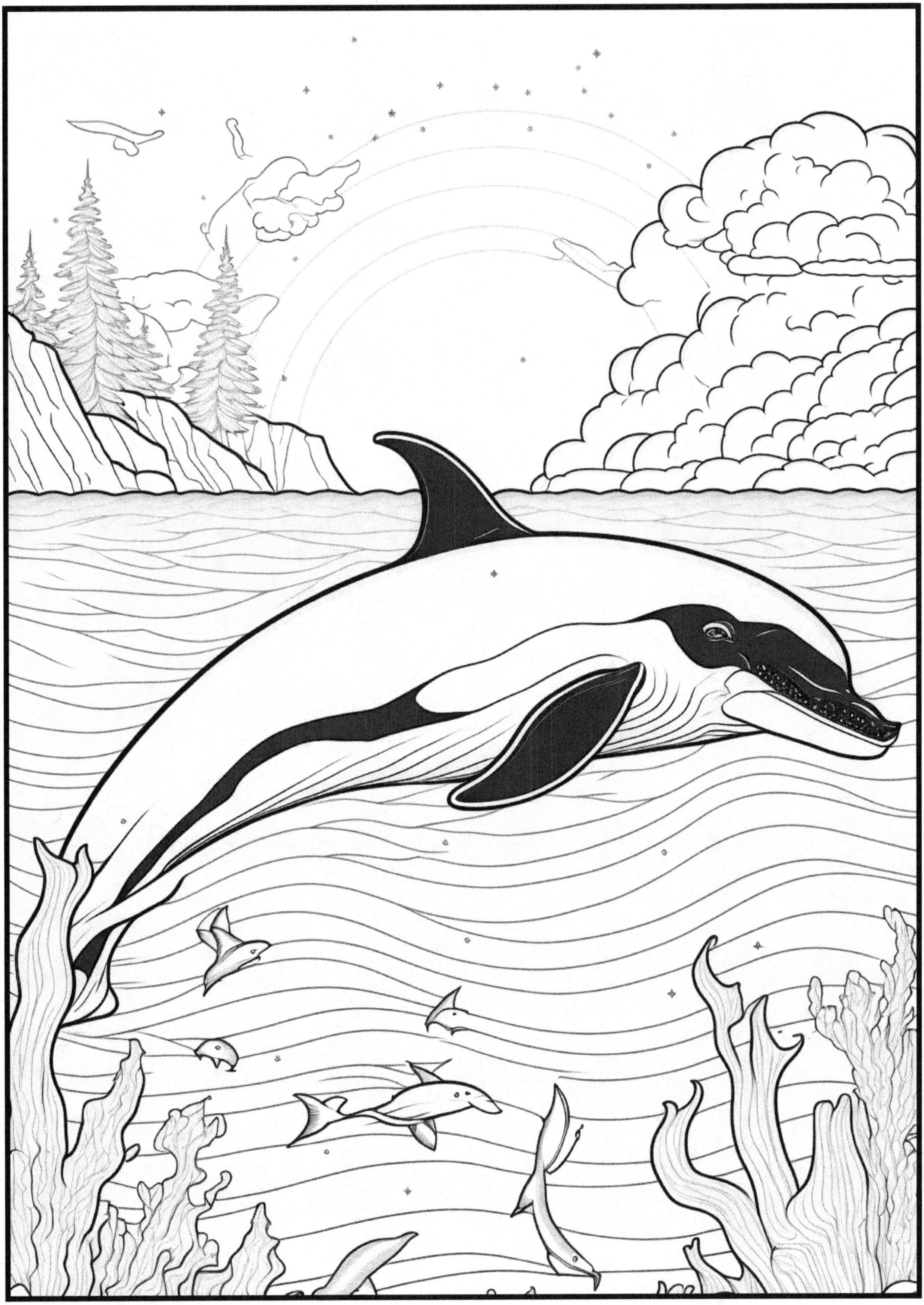

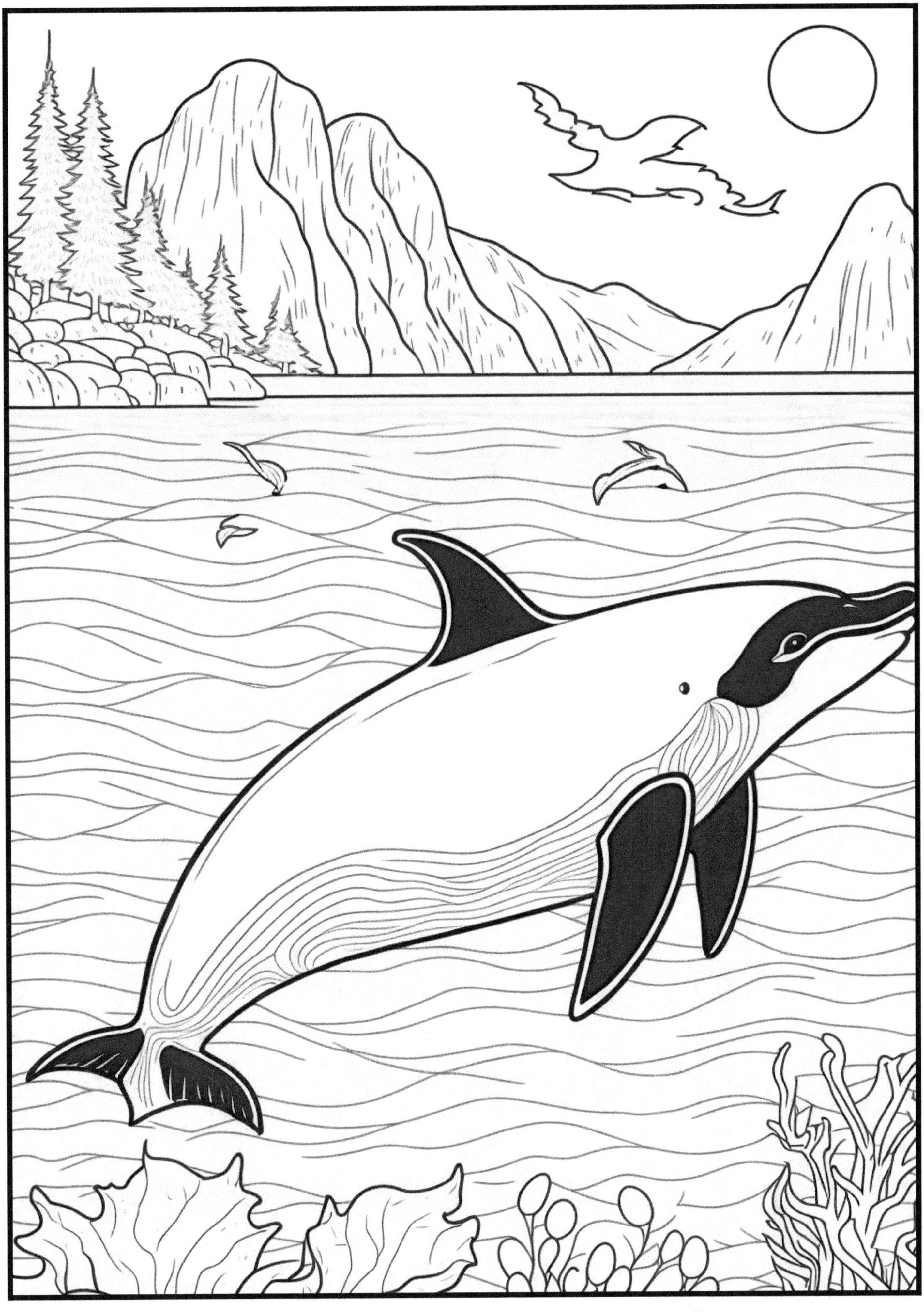

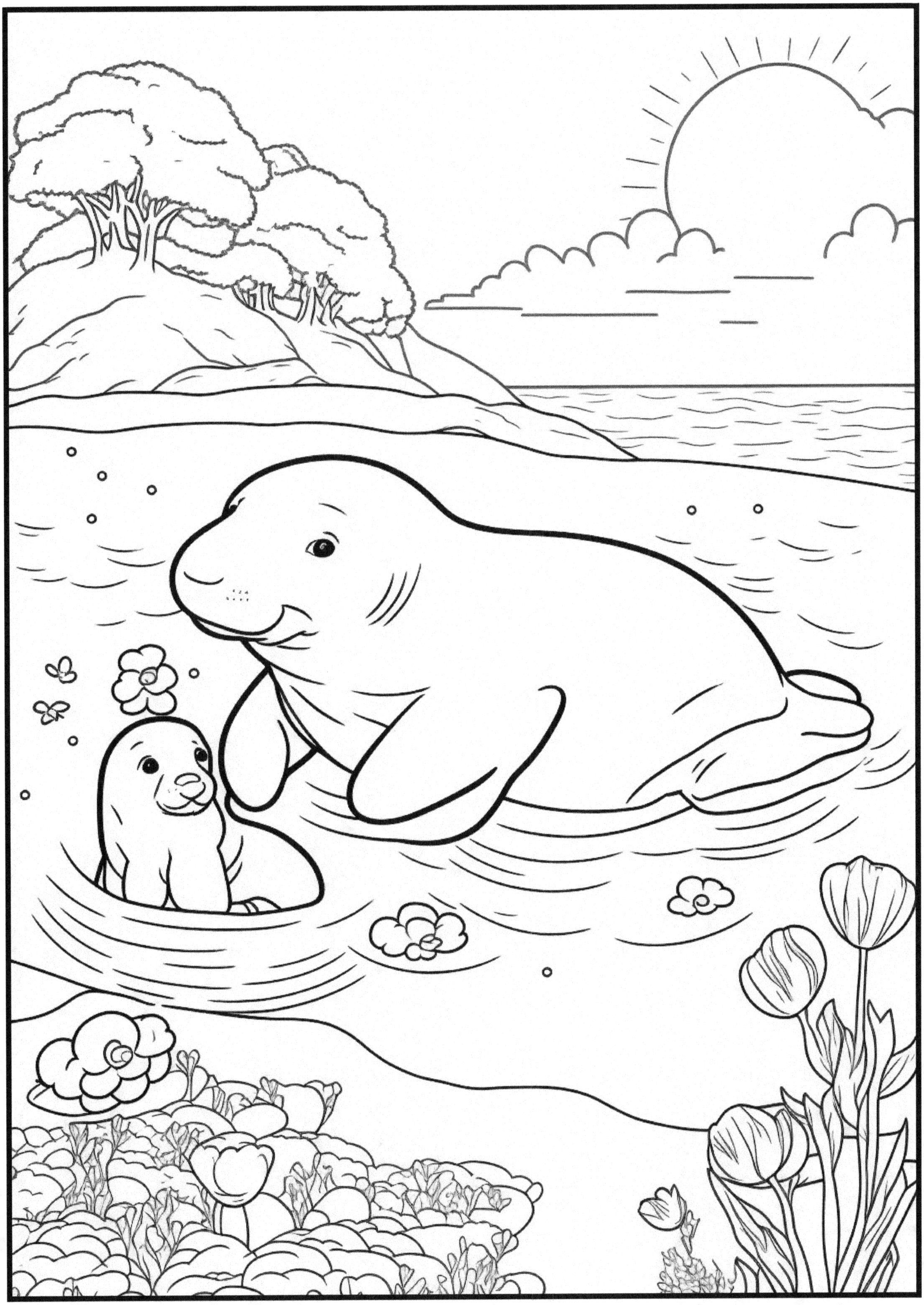

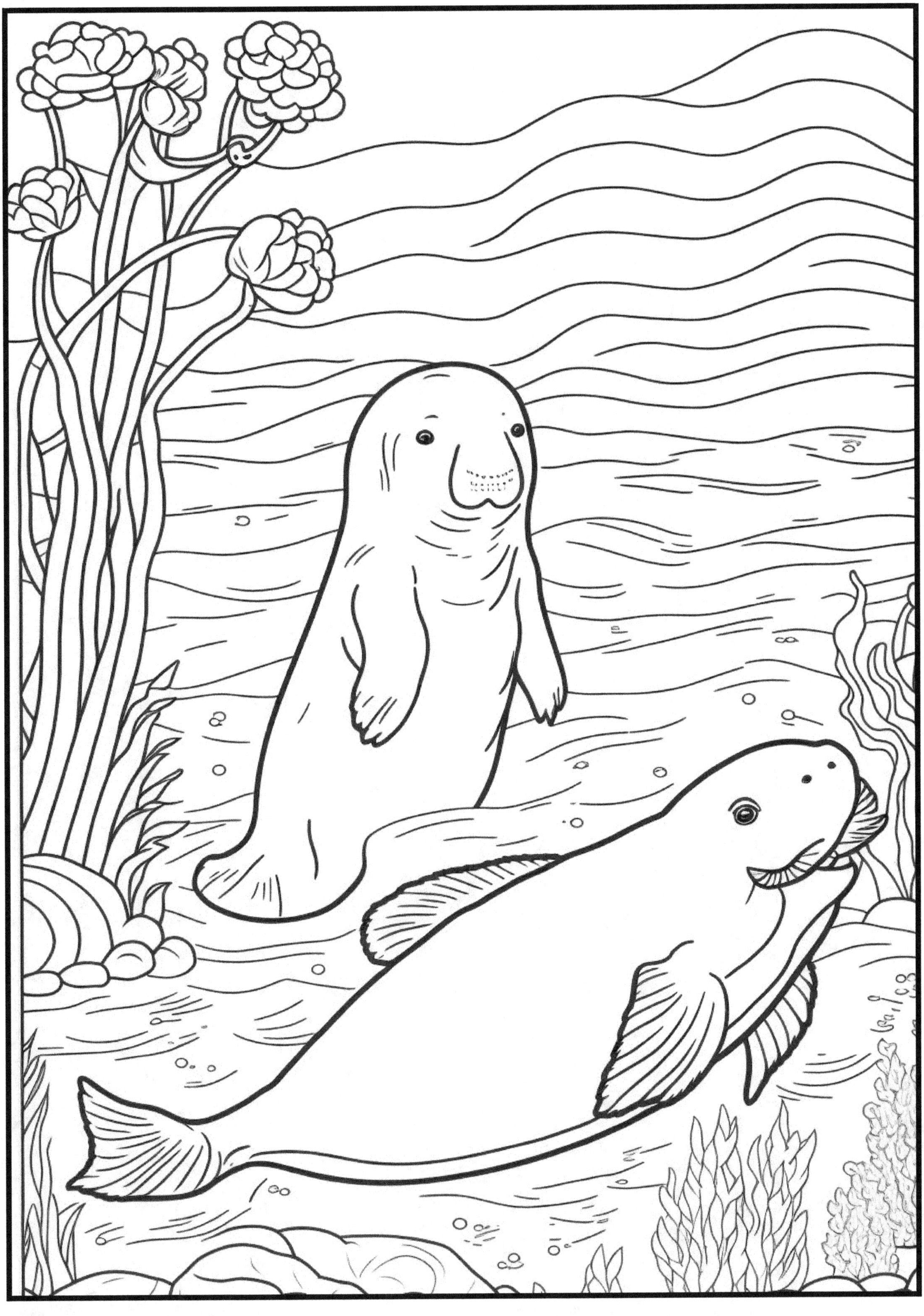

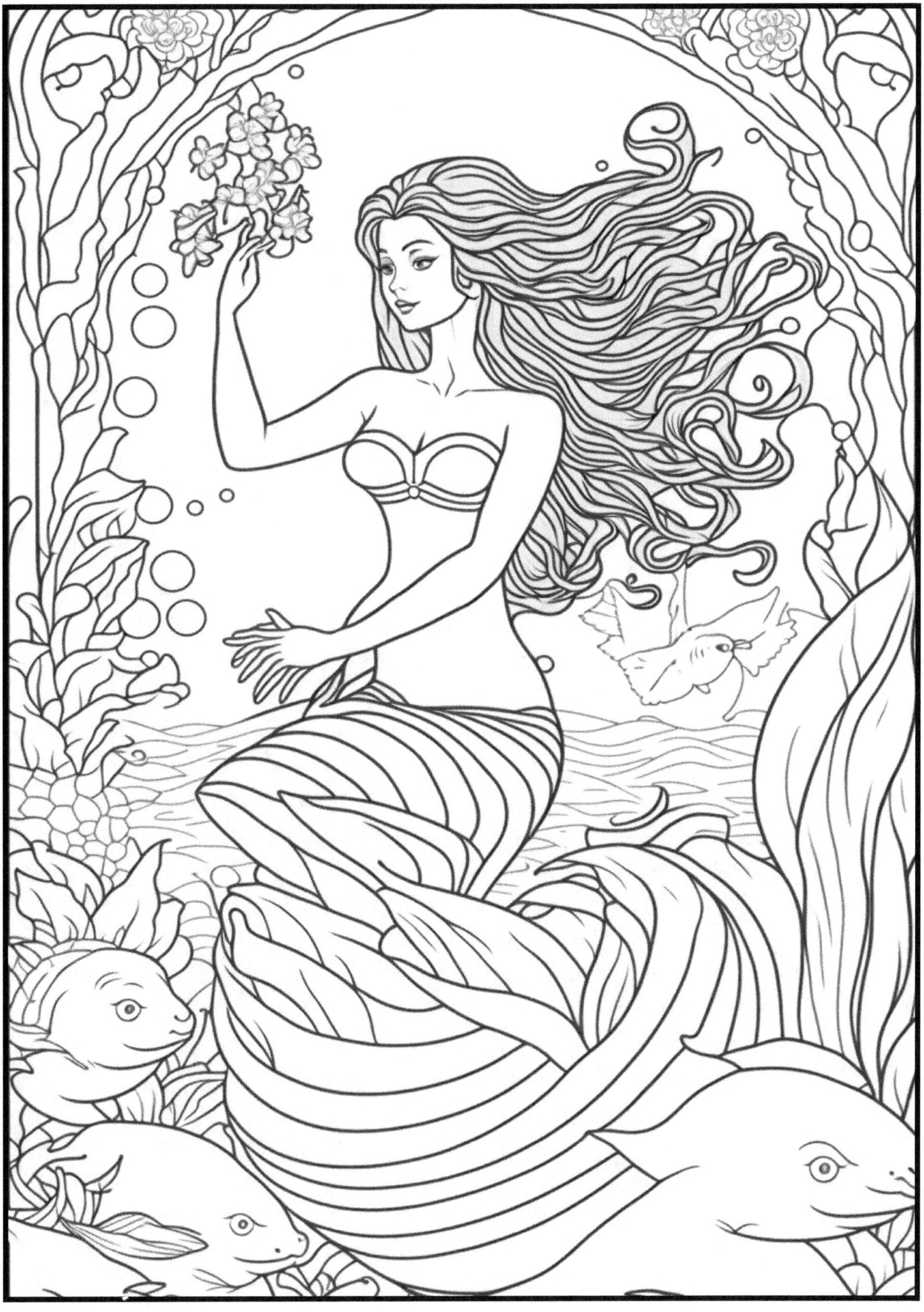

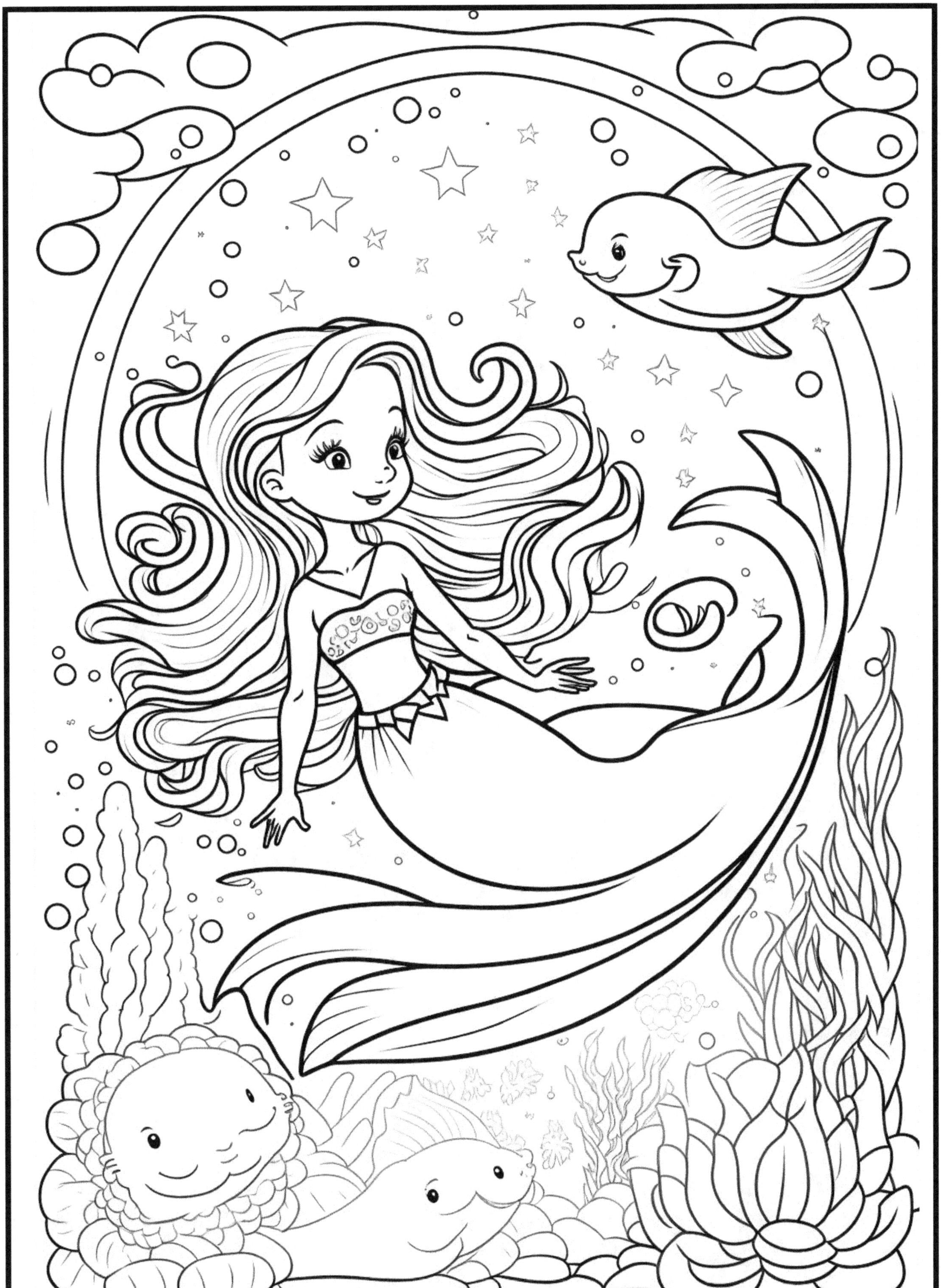

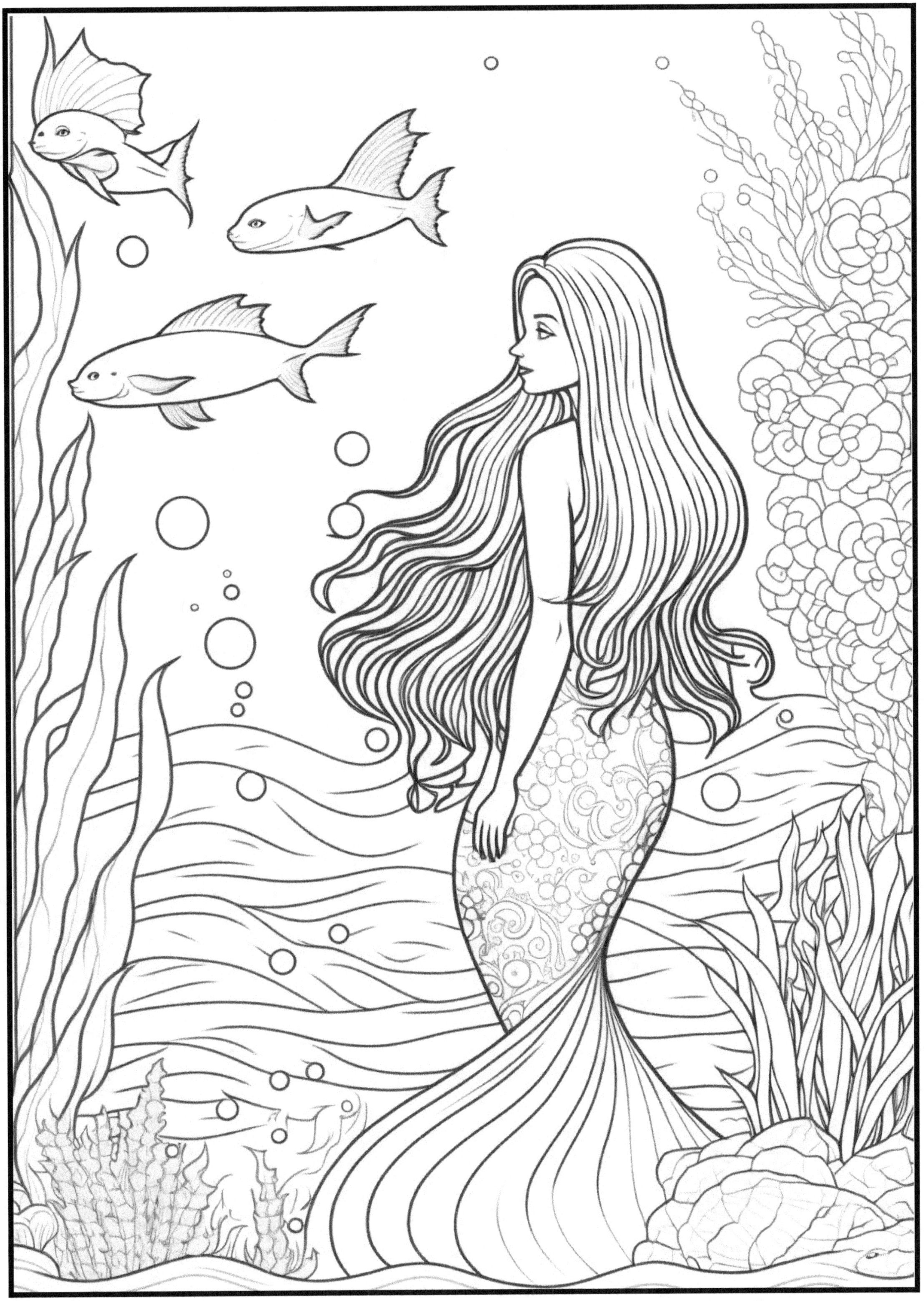

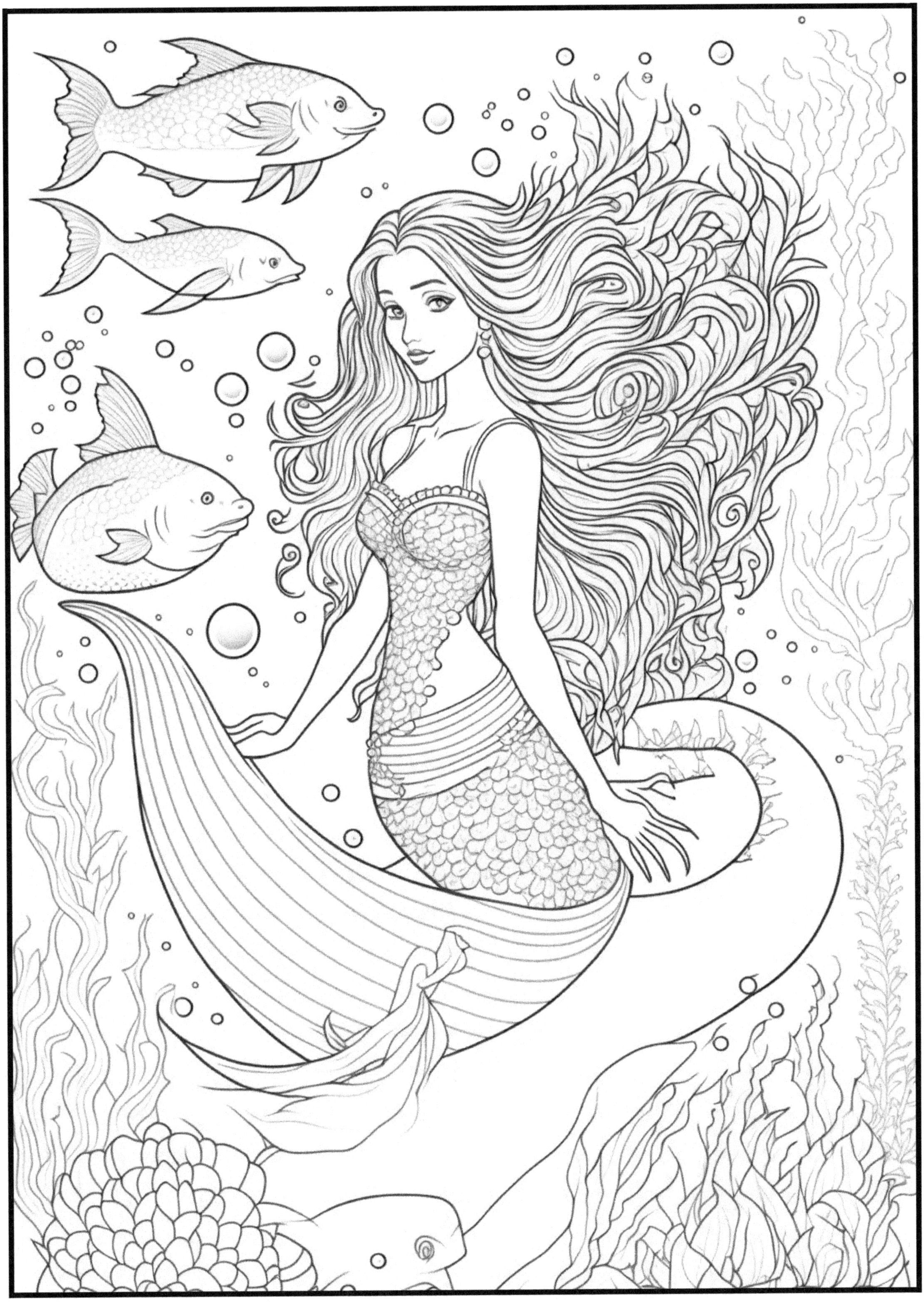

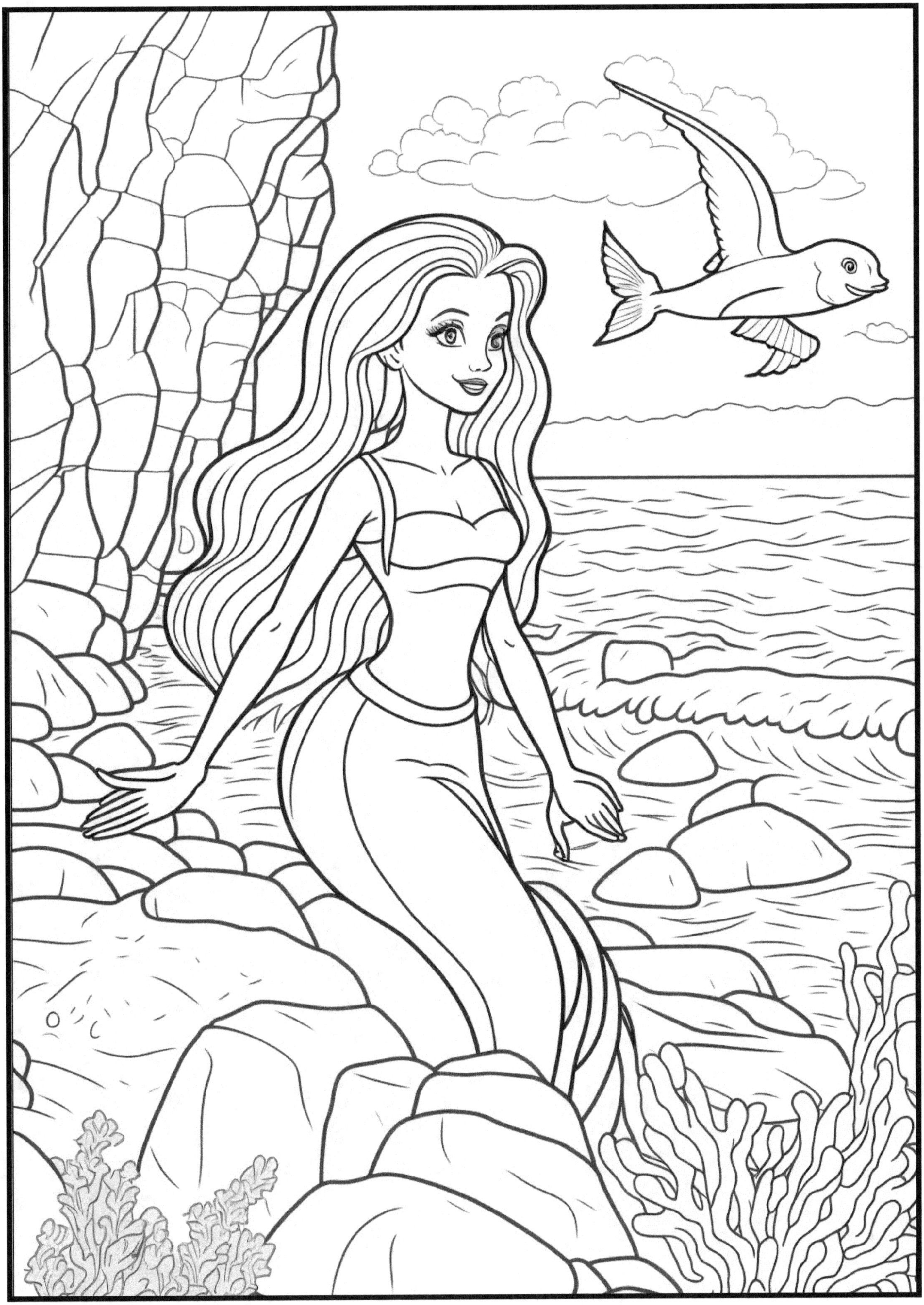

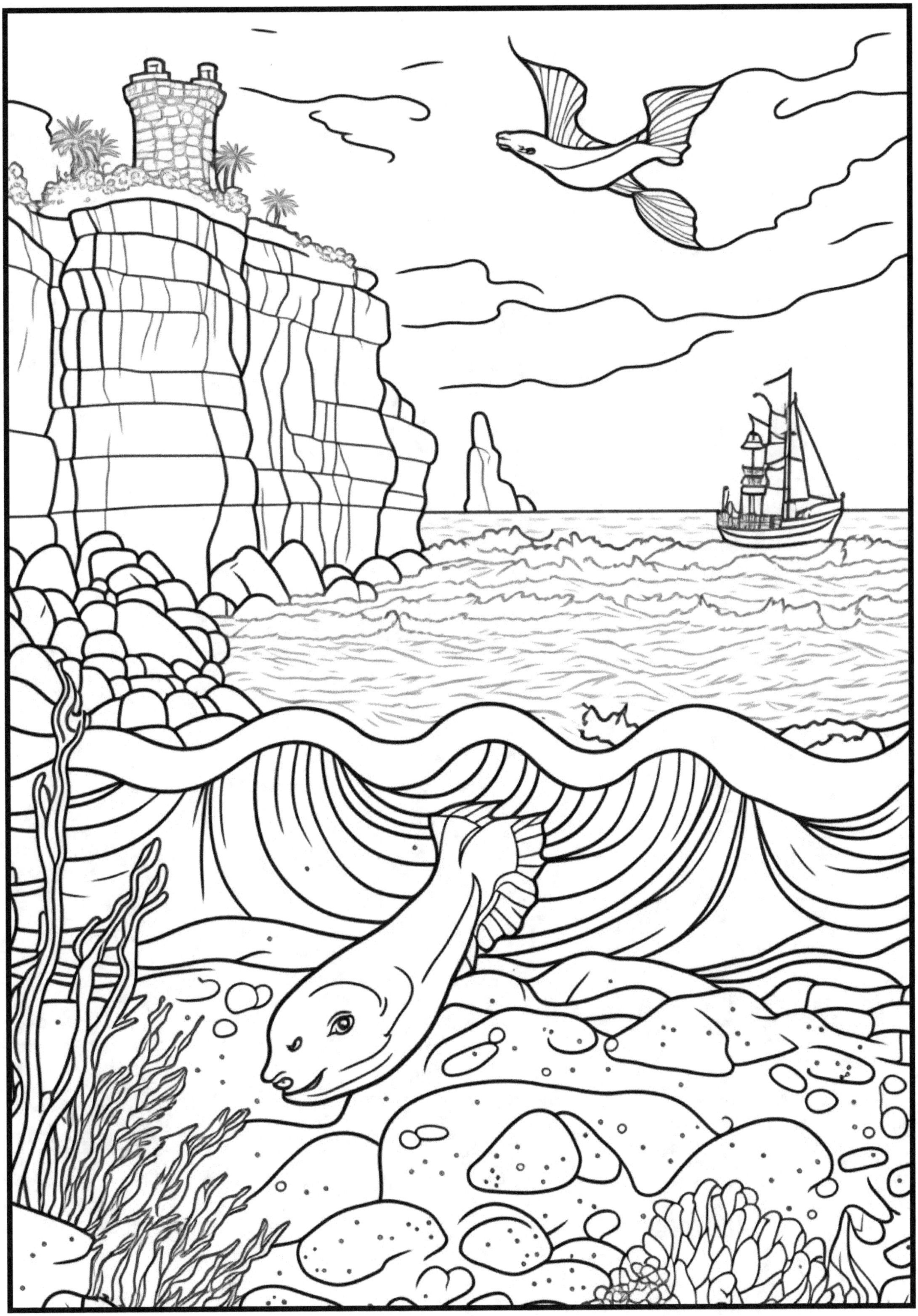

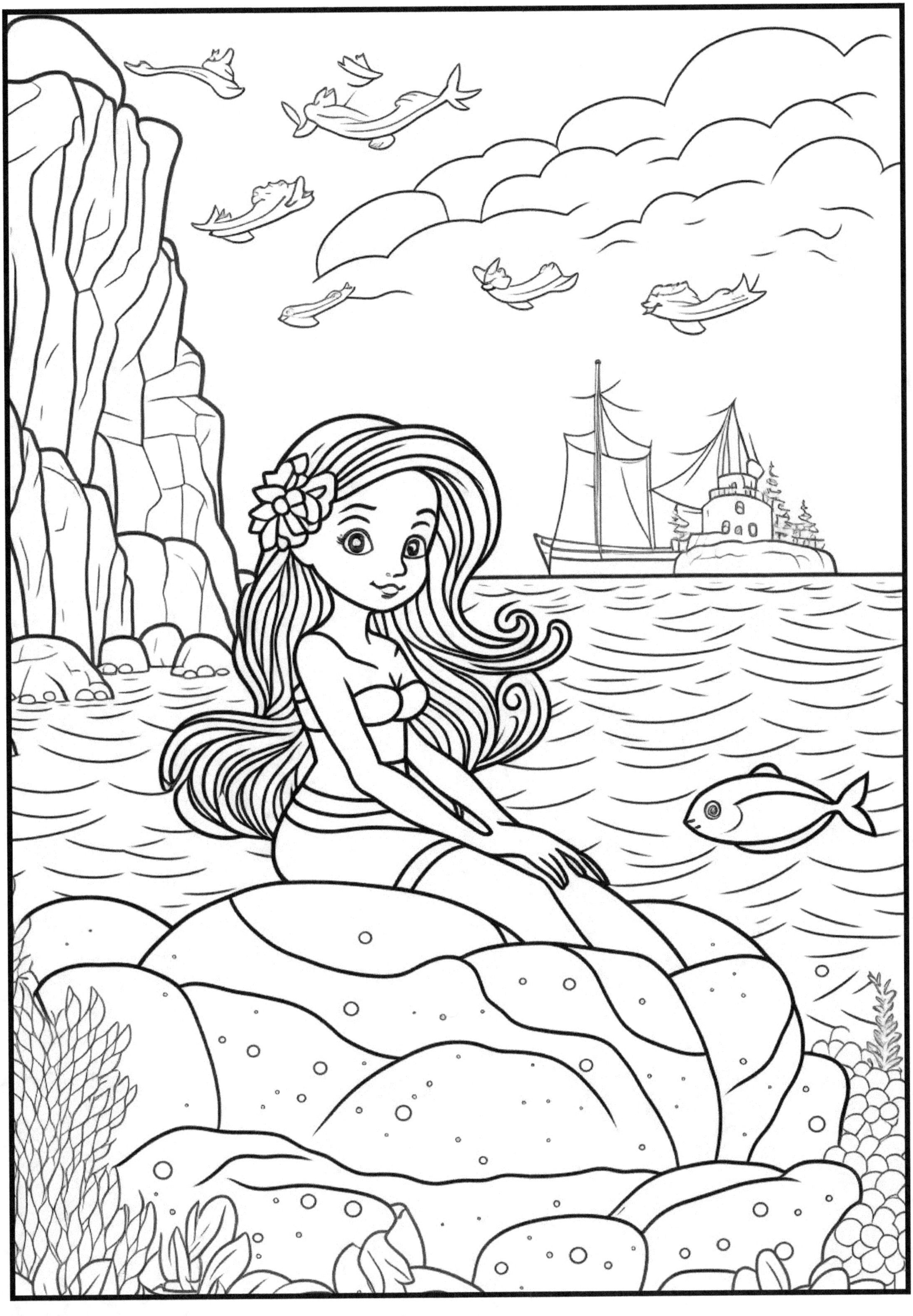

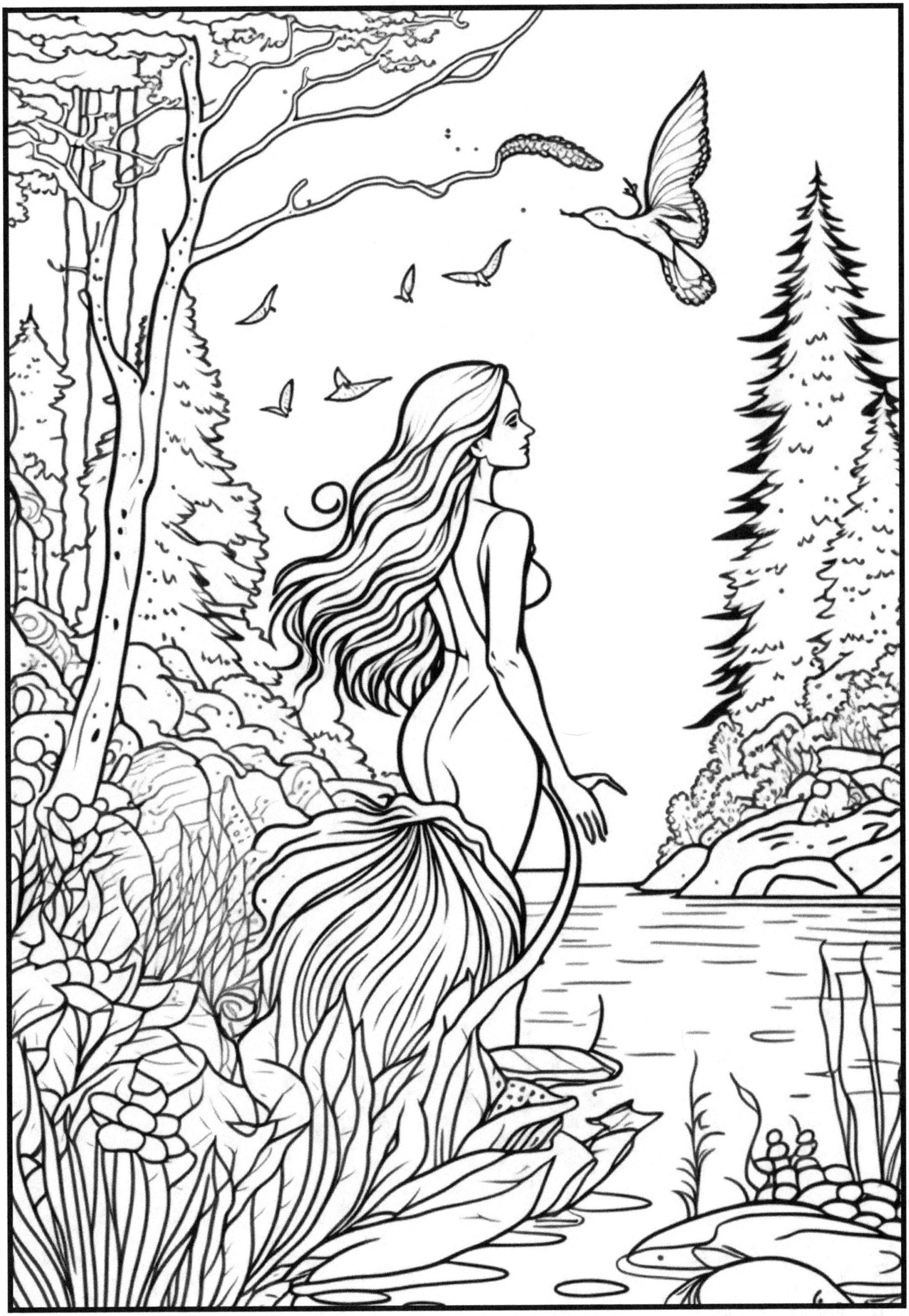

www.ingramcontent.com/pod-product-compliance
Lightning Source LLC
Chambersburg PA
CBHW062011220526
45467CB00032BA/2446
* 9 7 9 8 3 7 7 2 3 3 5 3 4 *